Praise for *Flavors Beneath the Canopy*

"When chefs share their stories and inspirations like Chef Oscar does in *Flavors Beneath the Canopy*, the industry moves forward. This mouthwatering celebration of Latin American cuisine preserves tradition, sparks new ideas, and belongs in every cookbook collection."

—John Doherty, chef-owner of BLACKBARN Restaurant, recipient of the James Beard Silver Spoon Award

"Chef Oscar's recipes carry the spirit of our ancestors while embracing the excitement of Latin American cooking. As someone of Latin heritage, I'm proud to champion a book that honors our culture with such authenticity, creativity, and heart."

—Derek Bugge, chef consultant; winner, Food Network's Guy's Grocery Games

"Chef Oscar's cookbook vividly captures the heart of Latin cooking—diverse, soulful, and deeply connected to fresh ingredients. The recipes are simple yet inventive, honoring tradition while inviting creativity. It's honest food, beautifully expressed, and a joy to cook from."

—Abraham Salum, chef and restaurant owner of Salum Restaurant, Dallas, Texas

"Jaguar always feels like home to me, with Oscar's exquisite dishes tasting just as remarkable as they did the very first time I had them. This cookbook brings that same spirit to life—capturing the family memories, celebrations, and the joy of sharing great food with the people you love."

—Gabriela Rivero, a leading voice in Miami's culinary scene

"*Flavors Beneath the Canopy* feels like a seat at Chef Oscar's table—full of heart, culture, and serious *sabor*. You can taste his journey from Mexico City to Miami in every recipe and feel it in the stories that turn a meal into a memory. This is the kind of cookbook that makes you want to gather your people, cook with love, and return to it again and again."

—Marivette Navarrete, founder/CEO of *The Mujerista*

FLAVORS Beneath the CANOPY

RECIPES INSPIRED BY LATIN AMERICA'S LUSH & VIBRANT LANDS

Oscar del Rivero Owner of Jaguar Restaurant

With James O. Fraioli

Photography by Alejandra Urquiza

Skyhorse Publishing

Culinary Book Creations

Skyhorse Publishing books may be purchased in bulk at special discounts for sales promotion, corporate gifts, fundraising, or educational purposes. Special editions can also be created to specifications. For details, contact the Special Sales Department, Skyhorse Publishing, 307 Fifth Avenue, 4th Floor, New York, NY, 10016 or info@skyhorsepublishing.com.

Skyhorse® and Skyhorse Publishing® are registered trademarks of Skyhorse Publishing, Inc.®, a Delaware corporation.

Visit our website at www.skyhorsepublishing.com.

Culinary Book Creations® is a registered trademark of Culinary Book Creations, a Washington LLC corporation.

Culinary Book Creations LLC
www.culinarybookcreations.com

10 9 8 7 6 5 4 3 2 1

Library of Congress Cataloging-in-Publication Data on file.

Creative Director and Production Manager: James O. Fraioli
Interior and cover designer: Jen Montgomery
Interior artwork by Rawpixel and Shutterstock

Print ISBN: 978-1-5107-8607-3
Ebook ISBN: 978-1-5107-8810-7

Printed in China

To my father, whom we call "El Oso"—the creator of the Jaguar Family. Thank you for your endless support, motivation, and generosity. You are the original "Jaguar."

Contents

Introduction

If you've ever stepped into Coconut Grove—Miami's unique neighborhood that is both avant-garde and authentically warm and relaxed—you've likely discovered our beloved neighborhood restaurant, Jaguar.

Respected and revered for thousands of years, the jaguar has played an important role in the ecosystems of its natural habitat of Central and South America. It is this region of the world—the jaguar's range—that is the inspiration behind our restaurant and the food and drinks served within. This Jaguar spirit remainsalive in Latin American countries in one way or another. It represents strength, warmth, and resilience. It also represents our culinary creations.

With roots dating back more than twenty years, our family-owned gem has been serving up Latin American cuisine with a flair that is distinctly our own. From a concept that began with crisp and vibrant ceviches served by the spoon, to today's extensive menu, of which you'll find many wonderful and delicious dishes throughout this book, Jaguar captures the essence of Latin American flavors and traditions. And like most Latin cultures, what's equally important to us is that every guest who walks through our doors feels genuinely welcome, comfortable, and at home. We are relaxed and unpretentious—just like our food. Come as you are, and feel free to be yourself. We believe our efforts provide a great experience from beginning to end.

Now, let me take you back, before Jaguar, to my upbringing, my family, and my passion for cooking so you understand what gets me excited and why Jaguar—and this cookbook—are so important to me.

Colonia del Valle, Mexico

I was born in Mexico City in the summer of 1975. At the time, the city—like it pretty much is today—was a vibrant metropolis where I grew up and spent seventeen years of my youth. A blend of history and modern conveniences, Mexico City, if you haven't been, boasts Aztec ruins, colonial architecture, and bustling markets that smell of fresh tortillas, tropical fruit, and fresh meats roasting on spits. The city's rich culture shines through in its art, music, and mouthwatering cuisine, which has always found its way into our home.

I lived with my mother, along with my brother, José Eduardo, who was three years older than me. We all shared a quaint little apartment in del Valle. My dad, Eduardo, whom I will reunite with later in this story, worked in advertising. After divorcing my mother when I was four, he left Mexico City and moved to the sunny shores of Newport Beach, California.

Every day, at three o'clock in the afternoon, when my brother and I sauntered home from school, we were greeted by the enticing aromas of chilies, cinnamon, and cumin emanating from the kitchen. With sleeves rolled up and singing aloud, my mother and our housekeeper, Esperanza, who doubled as my mom's sous-chef, whipped up delicious four-course meals during my mom's extended lunch break. She worked as a production coordinator in the motion picture industry (film credits include *Dune* and *Titanic*), and her schedule was quite hectic. But despite her grueling twelve to fourteen hours a day in the production office, she always made time to cook in the kitchen while making sure we had plenty to eat.

We'd all sit down to fresh garden salads, featuring vibrant field greens and sun-kissed vegetables from the local farmers market. Savory soups often followed, whether it was my mom's legendary Caldo de Camaron, a Mexican shrimp soup bursting with shrimp, chayote squash, and carrots bathed in a silky broth made with chilies and stewed tomato, or her traditional Chicken Tortilla Soup, which she slow cooked with an aromatic broth enriched with the flavors of onion, tomato, chipotle peppers, epazote, and fried pieces of tortilla chips. Like a well-orchestrated restaurant, as soon as we finished our last spoonful of soup, we'd be introduced to the next course. Because my mom and Esperanza enjoyed grilling, we ate a lot of fresh fish, like our local snapper, which they'd cook over mangrove wood and charcoal to create a distinctive smoke that permeated the lightly salted fish. Other times, we'd bury our forks into Cochinita Pibil, a Mexican pork dish in which the pork is marinated overnight in a combination of annatto paste, orange juice, and garlic. My personal favorite was mom's Chilorio, a Sinaloan-inspired dish consisting of fried pork simmered in a fragrant chili sauce and seasoned with just the right amount of cumin, garlic, and oregano. And just when we thought we couldn't eat any more, our extravagant homecooked dinner would conclude with a classic dessert like creamy caramel flan or crispy churros dusted with cinnamon and sugar. And that's how we ate. It was important to mom that we sat down every day for a hearty, home-cooked meal. My brother and I also learned from our mother and Esperanza the importance of fresh, sustainable ingredients and sourcing local whenever possible. They also steered us away from sugary drinks. Instead of soda pop, we stayed hydrated with refreshing fruit waters, often consisting of freshly made lemonades or limeades. But it wasn't just our mother and Esperanza who were terrific cooks.

Our grandmother from our mom's side was equally gifted in the kitchen. I remember when we'd visit her on the weekends and holidays. She'd invite us out back to her patio, where tables were adorned with fresh-cut flowers and plates and platters piled high with what seemed like endless food. There were always hot and cold appetizers (tapas) to snack on, like zesty guacamole made with fresh lime, white onion, and cilantro, and perfectly charred octopus, which my grandmother sliced thin and served with crispy potatoes. We'd feast all day while celebrating our family and friends. We'd then return to the table for dinner, where we'd enjoy such favorites as tacos de lengua, elotes (grilled corn on the cob), tamales, pozole (hominy soup with meat), quesadillas, and chilaquiles. Cooking was my grandmother's passion, and her love, warmth, and spirit went into every dish she prepared—just like my mother and Esperanza. When Grandma wasn't cooking for us, she was cooking for parties and events in the neighborhood. I remember my mother sharing stories of how grandma cooked for days for a neighborhood party, buying, prepping, and making everything from scratch, including her legendary moles—the masterpiece of sauces in Mexican cuisine. She'd spend three days making these famous dishes that represent the fusion of Mexico's pre-Hispanic and European cuisines.

As my brother and I grew older—now teenagers—our home-cooked meals became less frequent. We were now in high school, which meant less time at home and more time hanging out with our friends. Instead of eating with mom and Esperanza, we now frequented the restaurants in the city where we could gather with our friends and girlfriends to eat, drink, and socialize. During our summer breaks, my brother and I would then fly to California to visit our father, who, unlike Mom, didn't spend much time in the kitchen. Instead of tables adorned with tacos, tostadas, tortas, enchiladas, and platters of carnitas and ceviche like we were accustomed to, he'd put out a simple tray of smoked oysters, anchovies, olives, wine, and tequila. For him, simplicity and convenience trumped laboring over a hot stove.

During my last year of high school, I was a complete night owl, bouncing from restaurant to restaurant, and bar to bar, now with my girlfriend in tow. I met her at school, and she enjoyed partying as much as I did during our senior year. I remember one evening when I persuaded her to sneak out of her house so we could spend the entire night canvassing the bar scene. That didn't bode well with her parents—or my mother. When I finally sauntered back to our apartment in the early morning hours, my eyes bloodshot and clothes reeking of stale beer, my mother had had enough. She felt I was walking on the wrong side of the tracks, so to speak. With our family sit-down meals no longer taking place, and with me not taking my last year of school very seriously, she threatened that if I kept up my frivolous behavior, she'd send me to go live with my dad in California. Figuring she was bluffing, I remember confronting her and saying, "Sure, I'd be happy to move. Just tell me when." And that's exactly what happened.

Newport Beach, California

When I arrived in Newport Beach with suitcases in tow, I was seventeen with Mexico City now in the rearview mirror. As arranged, I moved into a pleasant two-story stucco house with my father, who was now a top executive for an advertising firm that specialized in producing commercials for large companies, like Budweiser and McDonalds, that were looking to break into the Latin and Spanish market. My father's first order of business was to enroll me in school so I could finish my final year of high school, which I wasn't terribly excited about. Not only was I a fish out of water in Newport, but I didn't know anyone, and going to school with strangers was not how I wanted to spend my days on the California coast. Nevertheless, I plodded along while my dad kept his nose to the grindstone at work. When I wasn't in school, I naturally explored the beach scene. It didn't take me long to realize how terrific downtown Newport Beach was. I discovered a dynamic mix of upscale dining, fresh seafood, and fashionable eateries. Oceanfront spots with stunning views served gourmet cuisine, while local cafés and taco stands offered Southern California flavors and a bit of my homeland. The chic steakhouses and lively brunch spots were equally impressive. There was no doubt Newport's culinary landscape was as vibrant as its sunsets.

By the time I finished my final year of high school, my father decided it was time for him to open his own firm. As it turns out, a colleague of his told him about an advertising company with enormous potential in Miami that had just gone on the market. Knowing this could be his big break, my dad jumped at the opportunity. The next thing I knew, we were saying goodbye to California and saying hello to Miami.

Miami Beach, Florida

Settling into yet another new city—this one now feeling more permanent—my dad said it was time for me to find a job. Through a connection of his, I took a bookkeeping gig at a small law firm in Coral Gables. The money was decent, but I found my daily duties and responsibilities mundane. Tracking billable hours, managing expenses, and reconciling accounts weren't terribly exciting for a high school graduate, although I was very accurate and praised by my boss for my strong financial oversight, which helped keep the operation smooth and compliant.

Wanting a bit more freedom at my age, and a job that didn't confine me to a desk, I left the firm and applied for a job as a delivery driver for a local Chinese restaurant. This led to delivering pizzas for Little Caesars, then artisan pies for the upscale pizzeria Greenwich Village Café. Delivering pizzas for Greenwich was my silver lining because it ultimately led to my foray into the restaurant business.

When I wasn't out making deliveries for Greenwich, my boss would lead me around the restaurant showing me the guts of the operation, which centered around a large brick oven and the rustic pizzas being assembled out front. Before I knew it, I was witnessing Italian tradition and craftsmanship, all coming together with hand-stretched dough, premium ingredients, and perfectly charred crusts thanks to the nine-hundred-degree brick-fired oven, which was critical to cook thin, crispy pizzas in about ninety seconds. I observed with interest how the pies were made and baked, each pizza and its fresh ingredients delivering rich, smoky flavors in every bite. I was enthralled. I found the process extremely rewarding and fun, whether it was watching a seventy-two-pound Parmesan wheel get broken down, or the peeling and roasting of sweet Italian peppers. It didn't take long until I was spending less time out making deliveries, and more time helping the pizza makers inside. It didn't matter to me what I was doing; whether it was washing dishes, making sauce, or grating cheese, I was finally enjoying my work. That's when my boss pulled me aside one afternoon and said he saw a lot of potential in me—that I could really excel in the culinary field. He further encouraged me to explore culinary school.

Culinary School

At the time, Johnson & Wales University in Miami was renowned for its culinary, hospitality, and business programs. With campuses in multiple cities, including Miami, the institution emphasized hands-on learning and a career-focused education. Known for its top-tier culinary arts program, JWU prepared its students for real-world success in diverse industries, blending academics with experiential opportunities and industry connections. I couldn't wait to apply.

Thanks to JWU's connections in the culinary industry, which they strongly promoted, I secured two internships during my enrollment. The first was for Cheeca Lodge & Spa in Islamorada, Florida, in 1999. Oh, what an internship that was. I mean, who wouldn't want to intern amidst turquoise waters, towering palms, calm breezes, and the most exceptional dining experience embraced by a twenty-seven-acre oceanfront resort in the Keys? From Hollywood celebrities to US presidents, they all frequented Cheeca Lodge & Spa, and I was honored to be part of their food and beverage program.

My second internship led me out of the country, to Austria, where I went to work in 2001 for DO &

CO, a world leader in the gourmet entertainment business that catered to airlines, restaurants, lounges, hotels, and international events. DO & CO was, and still is, responsible for catering the Formula 1, and they've been doing so for more than seventy-seven seasons while serving VIP guests of the Paddock Club at nineteen Formula 1 Grand Prix in eighteen countries. Like my time at Cheeca Lodge & Spa, interning at DO & CO provided me with hands-on experience, bridging the gap between my culinary education and the professional world. I learned to build my skills in practical, meaningful ways while making many promising industry connections.

Four years later, having finished my curriculum and internships with JWU, I was armed with a bachelor's degree in the culinary arts. I also became a proud father.

It was during my third year in culinary school that I married a fashion photographer named Carolina, whom I had met years ago in Mexico City. In 2001, she gave birth to our son Alejandro. Two years later, we had another son whom we named Diego. We remained in Miami Beach, living in a house with a detached cabana that doubled as my brother's home. While my brother ended up moving in with us, our father relocated to Coconut Grove, about an hour away.

Looking back on those years of culinary school, while establishing my career and starting a family, I am amazed at what I had accomplished. I went from absolutely loathing school in my early years to graduating at the top of my class. I never missed a day of school and earned high marks at JWU. I even made the Dean's List and received a scholarship.

Another memorable moment at JWU—and probably the most significant event that shaped my future—was when we had to create a mock restaurant for our final school project. We had to come up with a name, concept, and menu, which all went into the assembly of a business plan for our establishment. I remember working late on sketches and trying to brainstorm various concepts after my wife and kids went to bed. One concept that clearly stood out to me featured a jaguar. The thought first stemmed from my father's car—a Jaguar—which he purchased because of his obsession with the animal. He told me the elusive cat represents power, strength, courage, resilience, and transformation. The jaguar also stands as a symbol of leadership, vision, and a connection to nature's primal forces.

One summer, when I was visiting my dad in California, he gave me a jaguar mask that he had picked up from an artist in Mexico. I still remember that mask. The next morning, on my way to JWU, I was eager to share my project—Jaguar Restaurant—with my teachers and classmates. It's funny, looking back on those years at culinary school, I remember the only person who was more excited than me about school and my Jaguar restaurant concept, other than my wife and my father, was my mother. She couldn't believe I loved school and cooking so much, especially given the amount of cooking I was exposed to growing up. Surely, I had taken it all for granted. My mom and dad were adamant I had bribed my teachers and bought my degree, but that wasn't the case. I genuinely and honestly loved learning and working with food. It had always been—and remains—a passion of mine. And I couldn't wait to see where food would take me.

Bringing Jaguar to Life

After stints working in hotels in Miami Beach, cooking for various restaurants in and around the city, and traveling throughout Mexico and Latin America to learn more about the cuisine, I landed a job as a sous-chef at Talula. Owned by a husband-and-wife team, the Miami chef-driven restaurant was innovative and took pride in preparing and serving comforting, contemporary dishes. Talula was where I really honed my culinary techniques while learning the business and management side of the restaurant.

Meanwhile, my father had remarried by this time. His new wife, Mariluz, was also from Mexico City. She had three children with my father. As it turns out, Mariluz had a brother and sister who were in the restaurant business back in Mexico. One day, my father invited me over for dinner. When we sat down at the table, he and my stepmom presented an idea they had been mulling over for some time, and they wanted my opinion.

"What about opening our own restaurant, right here in Miami?" my dad began. "With your restaurant experience, and Mariluz's brother and sister in the business as well, we could open a family restaurant that specializes in authentic Latin American food. Best of all, we could all work together as one unit."

Immediately, my mind raced back to my business plan and Jaguar Restaurant. I agreed a family restaurant would be a great next step, and I shared with my dad and Mariluz that because Miami was so diverse, we could honor that diversity with Latin American cuisine while showcasing the food as best we could, following timeless traditions, techniques, ingredients, and flavors. When I asked my dad what a good name for the restaurant might be, without any hesitation he hollered, "Jaguar."

After scouting various locations for our restaurant, we settled on Coconut Grove. The community was a favorite of my father's, and it was—and still is—the heartbeat for that part of Miami. At the time, building space was at a premium and the rents were exorbitant. We either had to buy or sign what hopefully would be a long-term lease with some sort of controlled rent. The next morning, my father said to me that for Jaguar to be successful, we needed to own the building. And that's what we did.

After acquiring a large building in the heart of Coconut Grove, we went to work building our vision. And, finally, in 2005, we opened the doors to Jaguar Restaurant.

We began introducing the community to our Latin American restaurant by serving grilled steaks and ceviches by the spoon. It was a very new and different concept at the time, especially for the residents who already had their favorite dining spots. They had a hard time embracing our "foreign" cuisine. Nevertheless, we did not waver. We kept featuring authentic Latin American dishes while offering plenty of friendly, "come as you are" hospitality. Fortunately, after a couple challenging years, the concept finally caught on and Floridians accepted us and now consider us the "cool place" to dine.

Today, Jaguar Restaurant continues to impress our guests while the dishes and drinks represent our homeland and the culture and cuisine we embrace. Not only are we considered a neighborhood classic, but we recently celebrated our twentieth successful year in business. Without question, we are proud of what we have accomplished and where we are heading. The future looks bright, and we are excited for what lies ahead. For me, as the executive chef and owner of Jaguar, this is a dream come true. And this cookbook, as you'll discover throughout the pages ahead, is an extension of that dream.

JAGU
jaguar

AR
jaguar

Latin America:
THE SOUL OF OUR CUISINE

There are places in the world where food is more than sustenance—it's memory, identity, and celebration. Latin America is such a place. As a chef, I have always believed the heart of any cuisine lies not just in its ingredients, but in its people, its stories, and its land. And no land pulses with more color, flavor, and life than Latin America.

Stretching from the high plateaus of Mexico through the volcanic valleys of Central America, sweeping down the Andean spine of South America, and scattered across the lush, rhythmic Caribbean, Latin America is not one place—it's many. A continent of contradictions and harmonies. Of old and new. Of earth and fire. It is a place where jaguars still prowl ancient forests, where women still grind corn on volcanic stone, where entire cultures are kept alive through the rhythm of the kitchen.

In writing this cookbook, I am not merely collecting recipes—I am tracing the lifeblood of a land where food is poetry, protest, and prayer.

Through the Heart of Latin America: Color, Culture, and Cuisine

Since the inception of Jaguar, my journey has never been limited to the confines of the kitchen. It spills into the fields where crops are grown, the forests where spices whisper their secrets, the rivers where fish shimmer in the sun, and the villages where grandmothers stir pots that hold the soul of a people. Nowhere have I felt a connection more deeply than in Latin America—a mosaic of lands where every meal tells a story, every spice sings a song, and every bite is a step through history.

From the rugged highlands of Mexico to the rainforests of Brazil, from the bustling markets of Guatemala to the rhythmic islands of the Caribbean, Latin America is an explosion of color, flavor, and life. The cuisine here doesn't merely nourish—it celebrates. It remembers. It resists. And most of all, it unites.

The Wild Heartbeat: Nature's Pantry

Before I ever tasted a mole that moved me to tears or learned the dozens of ways to cook plantains, I felt the land itself—lush, wild, generous, and uncontainable. Latin America's natural bounty is staggering.

The Amazon, that vast emerald lung of the earth, pulses with ingredients that the world is only beginning to discover: açaí, cupuaçu, camu camu, and countless others that hide behind Indigenous names and stories. On the coasts, vibrant fruits like guanábana (soursop), passionfruit, and mamey offer their sweet, tangy flesh like tropical candy. Cacao, the sacred seed of the gods, grows in pods that look like lanterns and hold within them the bitter magic that becomes chocolate.

And then there's the jaguar.

This magnificent creature—the inspiration behind our restaurant—is more than just the apex predator of the rainforest—it is a symbol of power, mystery, and reverence across the Indigenous cultures of Latin America. The jaguar is the spirit of the forest, often feared, always respected. In Mayan cosmology, this revered cat was believed to walk between the worlds of the living and the dead, guarding the night. When I cook in places where the jaguar still roams, I feel that same duality—light and shadow, spice and sweetness, heat and cool—reflected in the dishes that emerge from those lands. The jaguar, to me, is the wild heartbeat of Latin America's cuisine: beautiful, stealthy, exciting, and essential.

Corn, Beans, and the Sacred Triad

If the jaguar is the soul, then corn is the body. Known as *maize* throughout Latin America, corn is more than just a crop—it is a deity. From the ancient Olmec and Zapotec civilizations to the highland Quechua communities of Peru, corn has been revered, cultivated, and transformed.

As a chef, few things humble me more than watching women nixtamalize corn in Oaxaca, soaking it in lime to unlock both nutrition and flavor. The result? Masa—a dough that becomes tortillas, tamales, pupusas, arepas, and more. Each variation reflects not just a place, but a people.

In Guatemala, I tasted tamales colorados, wrapped in banana leaves, red with annatto and tomato. In Venezuela, I devoured arepas stuffed with black beans and sharp cheese, dripping with avocado. Corn connects the entire region, from the soft humitas of the Andes to the crisp chulitos of the Caribbean.

Alongside corn are beans and squash, forming what many call the "Three Sisters." This trinity nourishes both land and life, offering sustenance and sustainability. These ingredients are not mere side dishes—they are the foundation of entire civilizations.

The Keepers of Fire: Indigenous Wisdom

Without question, I owe my deepest gratitude to the Indigenous peoples of Latin America. Without them, there would be no culinary tradition to speak of—only ingredients without purpose, fire without meaning.

Indigenous communities across Mexico, Central America, the Andes, and the Amazon carry a knowledge of the land that is encyclopedic. They know which plants heal and which ones harm, which fish to catch during what moon, and how to smoke, ferment, dry, and season using only what the land provides.

In the Sierra Madre of Mexico, I cooked with Indigenous people who showed me how to prepare a rustic stew with wild herbs and dried chili. In the Peruvian Andes, I helped dig a pachamanca—a communal earth oven where meats and tubers are layered with hot stones and buried to cook slowly with smoke and love.

These aren't just recipes—they're rituals. Cooking here isn't about ego or innovation. It's about memory. About offering. About staying in harmony with the land and giving thanks before taking.

The Markets: Living Museums of Culture

If you ever want to feel the pulse of Latin America, go to its markets. In every city and village, from Cusco to Cartagena, from San Juan to San Salvador, markets burst with chaos, color, and life. Vendors call out their prices, musicians strum guitars, children dart between stalls, and the smell—oh, the smell! —is a dizzying perfume of grilled meats, ripe mangoes, fresh herbs, and hot dough.

I treat these markets like sacred spaces. I listen to what the grandmothers are buying. I ask the tamale vendors about their masa. I taste everything. These markets are more than just supply chains—they are cultural archives. You can learn more about a people by what they eat, what they sell, and how they cook than by reading a hundred books.

Caribbean Colors and Island Heat

The islands of the Caribbean are Latin America's rhythmic heartbeat, where African, Indigenous, European, and Asian influences mix like a perfect stew. You taste it in jerk chicken kissed by pimento wood smoke, in mofongo mashed with garlic and pork cracklings, in callaloo, ackee, and saltfish.

Here, food is a celebration. A resistance. A declaration of identity.

I remember a kitchen in the Dominican Republic where the cook danced while making sancocho, a rich stew of seven meats. "You can't cook if you don't feel the music," she told me. And she was right. Caribbean food isn't just about ingredients—it's about rhythm, about movement, about joy.

Spices, Heat, and the Language of Flavor

Each region of Latin America speaks its own dialect of spice. In Mexico, it's smoky ancho, nutty pasilla, fiery habanero. In the Caribbean, it's Scotch bonnet, allspice, thyme, and cloves. In the Andes, it's the floral heat of aji amarillo, the earthiness of huacatay.

But heat here isn't about machismo or pain—it's about layering. About teasing out flavors. About balance. In the Yucatán, cochinita pibil slow cooked in banana leaves, marinated with sour orange and achiote, is not just spicy—it's deep, fragrant, mysterious. In Trinidad, doubles—fried flatbread with curried chickpeas—explode with flavor, but never overwhelm.

I've learned to respect spice not as a weapon but as a tool—one that shapes, brightens, and defines.

Art on a Plate, Art on the Walls

Just as every dish in Latin America tells a story, so too does its art. From the ancient petroglyphs of the Taino in the Caribbean to the murals of Diego Rivera in Mexico City, the region is a canvas of resistance, identity, and beauty.

Food and art here are inseparable. They borrow from each other. Both are acts of creation, of survival, of memory. In Oaxaca, I saw Zapotec embroidery patterns reflected in sugar skulls for Día de los Muertos. In Bogotá, I watched as chefs plated food that looked like landscapes—using Andean potatoes, edible flowers, and rainforest herbs to recreate memory on a plate.

In every region, color reigns—bright reds, sunny yellows, deep greens, and ocean blues. Latin American cuisine, like its art, does not shy away from vibrancy. It embraces it.

From Street Food to Fine Dining: The Spectrum of Flavor

Whether it's a $1 taco from a roadside stand in Chiapas or a ten-course tasting menu in Lima, Latin American food is united by one thing: soul.

Street food here is unmatched—empanadas, tacos al pastor, ceviches, elotes, baleadas, pastelitos, and churros. It's fast, affordable, and brimming with flavor. It's also deeply local. A pupusa in El Salvador is not the same as one in Honduras, and even within cities, street vendors guard their recipes like family heirlooms.

On the other end of the spectrum, chefs like Virgilio Martínez in Peru or Enrique Olvera in Mexico City are taking native ingredients and traditions and transforming them into haute cuisine—without losing the heart. They work directly with farmers, foragers, and fishermen to create dishes that honor the past while shaping the future.

For me, it's thrilling to see the world finally recognize that Latin American cuisine is not just delicious—it's profound.

A Final Toast: The Future Is Flavorful

As I travel through Latin America, I see not just the past, but the future—young chefs returning to their roots, farmers reclaiming ancient grains, communities fighting to protect their land and knowledge. I see hope, sown in soil, served on plates, and shared at tables.

Latin America is not one cuisine, one culture, one people—it is many. It is infinite. It is a land where jaguars prowl and hummingbirds hover, where drums beat and molcajetes grind, where every dish is a love letter to the land and the people who've fed it for centuries.

As the owner and proud chef of Jaguar, I am endlessly grateful to walk in this colorful, flavorful world—one bite at a time.

Disclaimer

As a chef, I deeply respect the ingredients and techniques used throughout Latin America. I am constantly learning from each culture and country. If a recipe is not an exact representation of a national dish, it is because we enjoy being creative and catering to our local guests. Our modifications are never intended to disrespect or misuse any ingredient or technique; we simply "Jaguarize" them out of love and respect for the original inspiration.

Ingredients and Pantry

I find Latin American cuisine endlessly inspiring because of the profound role ingredients play in shaping its identity. Every dish tells a story, with ingredients like corn, chili peppers, beans, and tropical fruits acting as historical and cultural messengers. From the earthy depth of Peruvian potatoes to the vibrant brightness of Mexican tomatillos, these ingredients are far more than flavor—they are heritage. The use of cacao in mole or the sacred role of maize in tamales reflects ancient traditions that have endured for centuries. Each region adds its unique flair, often rooted in Indigenous, African, and European influences, creating a rich tapestry of tastes and techniques. Ingredients aren't just chosen—they're honored. In Latin America, cooking is an act of cultural preservation, and as chefs, we get to translate that through every meal. That's the magic of these ingredients—they connect us to the past while feeding the present.

Below, you'll find information about some of the ingredients, perhaps unfamiliar to you, that I use throughout this book: what they taste like, where to find them, and notes—where relevant—about their fascinating role in Latin American cuisine. This isn't meant to be an exhaustive list, but rather a quick primer on foods in my recipes that are specific to the regions where they grow

Achiote Paste

Achiote paste is a vibrant red seasoning made from ground annatto seeds, spices, garlic, and vinegar. Popular in Mexican and Central American cuisine, it imparts a rich, earthy flavor and vivid color to meats and stews. Often used in marinades, it's essential in dishes like our Cochinita Pibil (Slow-Roasted Pork), page 28.

Ground Achiote

Achiote also comes in a ground form. Derived from the seeds of the Bixa Orellana tree, anchiote is a vibrant red-orange spice known for imparting a subtle earthy, peppery flavor and a rich yellow-orange hue to dishes. Widely used in Latin American and Caribbean cuisines, it's a key ingredient in recipes such as our Llapingachos (Potato Cakes). Beyond its culinary applications, achiote has been utilized historically for body painting and as a natural dye in cosmetics and textiles.

Aji Amarillo Paste

Aji amarillo paste is a staple in Peruvian cuisine, crafted from the vibrant orange-yellow aji amarillo pepper. This pepper imparts a unique fruity flavor with moderate heat, measuring between 30,000 to 50,000 Scoville heat units (see page xxxv). The paste enhances traditional dishes like our Croquetas de Pescado Ahumado (Smoked Fish Croquettes), page 32, and our Camaron Nuevo (Shrimp with Nuevo Sauce), page 162.

Aji Panca Paste

Aji panca paste is another wonder of Peruvian cuisine, made from the mild, deep red aji panca pepper. It offers a sweet, berry-like flavor with subtle smoky notes. This versatile paste enhances dishes like our Croquetas de Pescado Ahumado (Smoked Fish Croquettes), page 32; Salteñas (Bolivian Chicken Empanadas), page 116; and Anticuchos Peruanos de Res (Peruvian Grilled Beef Skewers), page 102; adding depth without overpowering heat.

Banana Leaves

Banana leaves are versatile in cooking, serving as natural wrappers for steaming, grilling, and baking dishes, as well for dramatic presentation purposes. We like to use banana leaves when making and serving our Cochinita Pibil (Slow-Roasted Pork), page 28. Banana leaves also impart a subtle, earthy aroma to food and help retain moisture. Common in Latin American and Southeast Asian cuisines, they provide an eco-friendly, biodegradable alternative to synthetic materials.

Chili Peppers (see chart, page xxxv)

Latin American chili peppers, originating from regions like Mexico and South America, are integral to the area's cuisine, offering a spectrum of flavors and heat levels. Varieties such as Mexico's jalapeño and habanero, and Peru's aji amarillo, range from mild to intensely hot, enhancing dishes like salsas, moles, and ceviches. Beyond their culinary uses, these peppers hold cultural and historical significance and have been cultivated for thousands of years.

Choclo (Large Peruvian Corn)

Also referred to as Choclo desgranado or giant corn kernels, you can find Peruvian or Cusco corn in the frozen vegetable section of most Latin American supermarkets. These kernels are preferred when we make such dishes as Ensalada Celia (Celia's Salad), page 138, and Langostinos Encocados (Prawns from Ecuador), page 188, because they're chewier and have an enjoyable starchy, hefty texture. They're also readily available online.

Green Plantains

Green plantains are a versatile, starchy staple in many cuisines, including Latin America. We enjoy using green plantains because of their neutral flavor and because they absorb our seasonings well. They're ideal when making both savory and sweet preparations, such as our Jibarito (Plantain & Steak Sandwich), page 42; Empanadas de Verde (Plantain Patties Empanada), page 36; and Tostones Bacalao Belinda (Crispy Tostones Topped with Codfish Stew), page 60.

Hearts of Palm

Hearts of palm are the tender inner cores of certain palm trees, harvested primarily from regions in South and Central America. They offer a delicate, slightly nutty flavor and a crisp texture, making them versatile in various dishes like our Salmon Norma, page 180. Rich in fiber, potassium, and iron, they contribute to a nutritious diet.

Hibiscus Flowers

Hibiscus flowers, known for their tart, cranberry-like flavor and vibrant red hue, are versatile in many culinary applications. Commonly steeped to create refreshing teas like agua de Jamaica, they also enhance sauces, jams, syrups, and desserts, like our Maize Crème Brûlée, page 232. In Mexican cuisine, rehydrated hibiscus flowers are sautéed with onions and spices for fillings in tacos, quesadillas, and enchiladas, offering a unique, tangy taste.

Maiz Chulpe (Dried Corn)

This amazing crunchy dried corn from Peru (not to be confused with cancha, which is starchier), resembles an imploded popcorn kernel. It's one of our favorite ingredients at Jaguar, and a delicious snack I enjoyed as a young boy and still do. The flavor of Maiz Chulpe is intense with an unrivaled texture, making it a wonderful complement to our ceviches, particularly our Peruano Ceviche (Peruvian Style Ceviche), page 167, and Camaron Nuevo (Shrimp with Nuevo Sauce), page 162.

Masa Harina

Masa harina is a traditional Mexican flour made from dried corn dough that has undergone nixtamalization—a process where dried corn kernels are cooked and soaked in an alkaline solution, typically limewater, to enhance flavor and nutritional value. This process makes the corn more digestible and allows it to form a cohesive dough when mixed with water. Masa harina is the foundation for many staple dishes in Latin American cuisine, including our Cacha Cachapas (Savory-Sweet Corn Pancakes), page 70, and our Arepas (Handmade Corn Cakes), page 106. Available in white, yellow, and blue varieties, masa harina is gluten-free and offers a slightly nutty, earthy taste.

Mexican and Spanish Cheeses

Cheeses like Manchego, Oaxaca, and Panela offer diverse flavors and textures. Manchego, made from sheep's milk, has a firm texture and nutty taste. Oaxaca, a stretchy, string cheese, is mild and creamy. Panela is soft, fresh, and slightly tangy, often enjoyed in salads or grilled. As you'll soon discover, we like to incorporate a lot of different Latin American cheeses in our dishes, like our Queso Fundido (Melted Cheese), page 50, and our Quesadilla de Tres Quesos (Three Cheese Quesadilla), page 54.

Yuca Root

Yuca, also known as cassava or manioc, is a starchy root vegetable native to South America and widely cultivated in tropical regions. It has a mild, slightly sweet, and nutty flavor, making it a versatile ingredient in various culinary traditions. Yuca is rich in carbohydrates and provides essential nutrients such as vitamin C, potassium, and folate. However, it must be properly prepared—typically by peeling, soaking, and cooking—to eliminate naturally occurring toxins. You can also buy canned yuca that's already been cooked. Yuca is quite popular at Jaguar, and we'll use the root vegetable in such dishes as our Frituras Mixtas Jaguar (Rustic Jaguar Hash), page 88, and our Yucas con Mojo y Aji Amarillo Aioli (Crispy Yuca with Sour Orange Cuban Mojo and Aji Amarillo Aioli), page 64.

Chili Peppers

I consider chili peppers to be the soul of Latin American cuisine. They bring more than heat—they add depth, complexity, and character to every dish. From the sweet and mild poblano in Mexico to the fiery aji amarillo in Peru, each region showcases its own varieties, flavors, and traditions. Chilies are used fresh, dried, roasted, or ground, enhancing everything from sauces and stews to marinades and salsas. They reflect the bold, vibrant spirit of Latin cooking. Chili peppers are a cultural symbol—connecting us to our roots while igniting creativity in every kitchen across Latin America.

HABANERO
100,000–350,000 SHU
Floral, fruity, very hot
Salsas, hot sauces, marinades

CHILTEPIN
50,000–100,000 SHU
Sharp, smoky, very hot
Salsas, pickled, seasoning

AJI AMARILLO
30,000–50,000 SHU
Fruity, slightly sweet
Ceviches, sauces, stews

SERRANO
10,000–25,000 SHU
Bright, crisp, medium heat
Salsas, sauces, raw in dishes

GUAJILLO
2,500–5,000 SHU
Tangy, berry-like, mild heat
Moles, salsas, marinades

PASILLA
1,000–2,500 SHU
Rich, earthy, mild heat
Moles, soups, sauces

AJI PANCA
1,000–1,500 SHU
Sweet, smoky, mild heat
Marinades, stews, fish dishes

** SHU = Scoville Heat Units*

MALAGUETA
60,000–100,000 SHU
Pungent, slightly smoky, very hot
Sauces, soups, stews

ROCOTO
30,000–100,000 SHU
Juicy, thick-fleshed, very hot
Stuffed dishes, sauces, raw in salsas

CHILE DE ARBOL
15,000–30,000 SHU
Sharp, smoky, hot
Hot sauces, soups, stews

JALAPEÑO
2,500–8,000 SHU
Bright, vegetal, mild to medium heat
Salsas, stuffed peppers, pickled

MULATO
2,500–3,000 SHU
Sweet, chocolatey, mild heat
Moles, sauces, stews

ANCHO (DRIED POBLANO)
1,000–2,000 SHU
Sweet, raisin-like, mild heat
Moles, sauces, chili pastes

POBLANO
1,000–1,500 SHU
Mild, earthy, slightly sweet
Chiles rellenos, sauces, roasted

Helpful Tools and Equipment

Because I'm constantly in the kitchen, I strongly believe having the right tools and equipment is essential to delivering consistent, high-quality food. Good tools not only save time but also help maintain precision and safety. A sharp knife, for example, ensures clean cuts and reduces the risk of accidents, while a reliable thermometer guarantees food is cooked to the correct temperature, protecting both flavor and health. Equipment like mixers, food processors, and blenders allow us to work efficiently, especially during busy services when every second counts. Specialized tools can also elevate dishes by enabling techniques that wouldn't be possible otherwise. Having helpful equipment can also reduce physical strain, making the kitchen a more sustainable environment for long-term work. Ultimately, the right tools empower the chef to focus on creativity and execution, ensuring every plate meets the highest standards, whether cooking at a restaurant or at home. It doesn't matter if I'm cooking for four or forty, a well-equipped kitchen is the foundation for culinary excellence and a more enjoyable cooking experience.

Below is a list of some of the important tools and equipment I use on a regular basis, and that you should also have available, especially when making the various drinks and dishes in this book.

Basic Barware

Essential bar tools like a muddler, shaker, and strainer are important when crafting our cocktails. A muddler extracts essential oils and aromas from fruits and herbs, enhancing their depth of flavor. A shaker mixes ingredients thoroughly, ensuring consistency. And a strainer filters out solids, delivering a smooth, refined beverage.

Blender

A kitchen blender is essential for efficient meal preparation, enabling quick blending, pureéing, and mixing of ingredients. It saves time, enhances texture, and supports healthy eating by facilitating the incorporation of fruits and vegetables into daily meals.

Candy Thermometer

A candy thermometer is essential for precise temperature measurement when deep-frying. It ensures accurate cooking temperatures, helping achieve desired textures and prevent burning. With a higher temperature range than meat thermometers, it typically measures up to 400°F. Using a candy thermometer also enhances safety and consistency in high-temperature cooking.

Cast-Iron Skillets

Cast-iron skillets are valued for their durability, excellent heat retention, and versatility in cooking. We use them all the time at Jaguar. They also develop a natural nonstick surface when properly seasoned, enhancing cooking performance. Suitable for various heat sources, including stovetops and ovens, they can last for generations with proper care.

Dutch Oven

A Dutch oven is a versatile, heavy-duty pot essential for slow cooking, braising, baking, and frying. We use it often when frying our calamari or making our Chamorritos con Salsa (Three Chiles Glazed Pork Shanks), page 26; Chilaquiles Rojos (Fried Corn Tortillas with Red Salsa), page 72; or Panceta de Cerdo Brasileña con Frijoles Negros, Mandarina Encurtida, y Farofa (Pork Belly Brazil with Black Beans, Pickled Mandarin Relish, and Farofa), page 216. The Dutch oven also boasts excellent heat retention and even distribution, making it ideal for tenderizing tough cuts of meat and baking crusty breads. Available in various sizes and designs, a Dutch oven is a valuable investment for any kitchen.

Food Dehydrator

A food dehydrator, if you're not familiar, preserves food by removing moisture and extending the ingredient's shelf life without refrigeration, but still retains the nutrients and flavors, offering healthy snacks without additives. Dehydrating also reduces food waste and saves money by prolonging edibility. Food dehydrators are energy efficient and free up oven space for other cooking tasks. This piece of equipment comes in handy at Jaguar, especially when we're dehydrating fruit wheels for our cocktail garnishes.

Food Processor

A food processor streamlines kitchen tasks by chopping, slicing, shredding, and mixing ingredients rapidly. It ensures consistent results, simplifies meal preparation, and saves time, making it indispensable for both novice and experienced cooks.

Immersion Blender

Like the food processor, an immersion blender also streamlines cooking by puréeing soups directly in pots, blending small quantities efficiently, and emulsifying dressings and sauces. Its compact design simplifies storage and cleanup, making it a versatile tool that saves time and reduces the need for multiple appliances.

Instant Pot

An Instant Pot combines multiple cooking functions—pressure cooking, slow cooking, sautéing, and more—into one appliance, streamlining meal preparation. It significantly reduces cooking times, making it convenient for busy lifestyles. Its versatility and efficiency make it a valuable addition to any kitchen. We always reach for the Instant Pot when we make our Pure de Frijol (Black Beans & Purée) page 48.

Mortar and Pestle

A mortar and pestle are timeless kitchen tools used for grinding and crushing ingredients for dishes like our fresh guacamole, page 40. Crafted from stone, ceramic, or wood, the mortar and pestle allow cooks to manually process herbs, spices, and garlic, releasing their full flavor and aroma. Unlike electric grinders, this age-old tool offers greater control and a rustic touch while connecting traditional cooking methods with modern culinary creativity in a simple yet powerful way.

Outdoor Grill

An outdoor grill enhances culinary experiences by providing a dedicated space for cooking and entertaining outdoors. It offers a convenient cooking center, reducing indoor heat and odors. Grilling often leads to healthier meals, as excess fats drip away. Additionally, outdoor grilling encourages spending more time outdoors, benefiting mental well-being.

Welcome to Our Family Table

Welcome to our table, where warmth is at the heart of every dish and every flavor tells a story. In the following pages, I invite you into the vibrant, soulful world of Latin American cuisine, not just as a collection of recipes, but as a celebration of family, friendship, and heartfelt hospitality.

These are the meals that bring people together: dishes passed down through generations or inspired by our Jaguar guests, shared over laughter, milestones, and quiet Sunday afternoons. Latin American cooking is about connection—the scent of slow-simmered mole, the hiss of tortillas on the comal, or the comforting warmth of pozole bubbling on the stove all carry memories of home.

Here you'll find recipes for drinks and dishes that awaken the senses and feed the soul. Whether you're cooking for a holiday feast or a simple dinner, every recipe is designed to bring people closer. You don't need fancy tools or hard-to-find ingredients, just a love of good food and the desire to share it.

My hope is that these dishes inspire you to create your own memories, stories, and traditions around the table—because food, at its best, is meant to be shared.

Should you have any questions, or if a recipe doesn't turn out quite as you expected, please reach out to me through the Jaguar Restaurant Instagram or YouTube account. I'll be happy to help. I may even create a video walking through the dish or recipe in more detail.

POTIONS & BITES

At Jaguar, we enjoy bringing the vibrant flavors of Latin America to life through our hand-crafted cocktails and mouthwatering appetizers. With a deep love for the region's rich culinary traditions, we create dishes that are both authentic and inventive. From our tempting ceviches and Queso Fundido to our savory Smoked Fish Croquetas and Tacos de Pacholas, the appetizers you will discover in this lively chapter burst with bold, fresh ingredients and unforgettable flavor.

Complementing these bites are our marvelous cocktails, many made with Latin America's iconic spirits like cachaça, mezcal, pisco, and rum. Whether it's a classic Caipirinha or a smoky Mezcaltini, our drinks are perfectly balanced to refresh and delight.

Together, our cocktails and appetizers offer a true taste of Latin American hospitality—festive, flavorful, and full of heart. With every sip and bite, we invite you to experience the passion, warmth, and culinary richness of both Jaguar and a region that knows how to celebrate through food and drink.

Besos de Fresa

STRAWBERRY KISSES

When it comes to summer cocktails, either at home or at Jaguar, this bright, delicious drink is one of my favorites because of its vibrant color and refreshing taste. I call this cheerful sipper Besos de Fresa, meaning "strawberry kisses," and making one of these beauties from scratch is a breeze. It requires fresh muddled strawberries, London gin, fresh lime juice, and St. Germain, which is an elderflower liqueur. When making, shake and don't blend. Then add some house-made strawberry purée and simple syrup and top it off with bubbly for that effervescent finish.

Makes 4 cocktails

STRAWBERRY PURÉE
Makes about 1½ cups

¾ pound fresh strawberries, washed, hulled, and quartered

Cane sugar, as needed, optional

SIMPLE SYRUP
Makes 4 cups

4 cups water

4 cups cane sugar

RIM
Lime wedges and cane sugar

OTHER
8 fresh strawberries plus more for garnish, washed and hulled

1 cup London dry gin

½ cup fresh lime juice

½ cup St. Germain Liqueur

½ cup Strawberry Purée

¼ cup Simple Syrup

Sparkling wine, as needed

To make the Strawberry Purée: Add the strawberries to a saucepan and simmer over very low heat for about 15 minutes, or until the strawberries are broken down (this process enhances the flavor). Remove the berries from the pan and let cool. Then add to a bar or kitchen blender, and blend until smooth and puréed. You can add a little sugar if you feel the strawberries aren't sweet enough, usually between 1 teaspoon and 1 tablespoon, depending on the berries and how sweet you'd like your purée to be. Bottle and refrigerate until needed, or up to 1 week.

To make the Simple Syrup: Add the water to a pot over high heat and bring to a boil. Once boiling, remove from the heat and add the sugar. Stir until completely dissolved. Let sit until the syrup reaches room temperature. Then bottle and store in the refrigerator until needed, up to 1 month.

Run fresh lime wedges around the rim of 4 tall (highball) glasses. Then roll the moistened rims in cane sugar. Add 2 strawberries to each glass. Using a muddler, gently yet firmly muddle the berries to release their juice, then add a handful of ice to each glass. Set the glasses aside.

Add the gin, lime juice, St. Germain, strawberry purée, and Simple Syrup to a shaker with ice. Shake for 8 seconds, strain into the prepared glasses, top with sparkling wine, garnish with fresh strawberries, and serve.

Caipirinhas

CLASSIC, IPANEMA & RIO

Welcome to Brazil's national cocktail—the Caipirinha. This beloved classic, which originated in the countryside of São Paulo in the early 20th century, is simple and vibrant. Initially consumed as a remedy for the common cold, the Caipirinha, which evolved into a symbol of Brazilian culture and embodies the country's zest for life and celebration, is enjoyed around the world. Our delicious concoction features cachaça, a sugarcane spirit, muddled lime, and homemade simple syrup, which we shake with some extra lime juice. The result is a cold, citrusy drink with a hint of sweetness and a kick from the cachaça. We also like to add some fruit purée to our Caipirinha, offering our guests variations on the famous beverage. We'll substitute the simple syrup with passion fruit purée for an Ipanema Caipirinha or replace the syrup with mango purée for the Rio Caipirinha.

Makes 4 cocktails

CLASSIC
Makes 4 drinks

2 limes, cut into quarters
1 cup cachaça
½ cup fresh lime juice
½ cup Simple Syrup (page 2)
½ cup passion fruit purée
½ cup mango purée

Add 2 lime segments to 4 tall (highball) glasses. Using a muddler, gently yet firmly muddle the limes to release their oils and juice, then add a handful of ice to each glass. Set aside.

Add the cachaça, lime juice, and Simple Syrup to a large cocktail shaker filled with ice. Shake vigorously for 8 seconds. Strain into the prepared glasses, gently stir, and serve.

For an Ipanema Caipirinha, replace the simple syrup with ½ cup Passion Fruit Purée. For a Rio Caipirinha, replace the simple syrup with ½ cup Mango Purée.

Brazil's Cachaça

As the owner of Jaguar, I've poured countless spirits, but few carry the soul and story that cachaça does. Born in Brazil over five hundred years ago, cachaça is the country's national spirit, distilled from fresh sugarcane juice—unlike rum, which typically uses molasses. It emerged during the colonial period when Portuguese settlers brought sugarcane to Brazil. Enslaved Africans discovered the fermentation potential of the sugarcane froth, and the distillation process soon followed, creating what we now know as cachaça.

It's the backbone of Brazil's iconic cocktail, the Caipirinha, a refreshing mix of cachaça, lime, and sugar that's become a global favorite. But cachaça isn't just for cocktails. With over four thousand brands in Brazil and varieties aged in native woods like amburana or bálsamo, it offers a complexity that rivals fine whiskey or tequila.

In recent years, cachaça has gained international popularity, thanks to craft distilleries and global interest in authentic, regional spirits. Behind every pour is a piece of Brazil's culture—its rhythm, resilience, and passion. When we serve a cachaça-based drink at Jaguar, we're not just offering alcohol, we're sharing a centuries-old tradition that continues to evolve and inspire.

Costa Verde

THE GREEN COAST

The Costa Verde is a delightful sip of paradise, capturing the essence of the coastal lifestyle in Brazil with its crisp flavors and invigorating aroma. At Jaguar, we assemble a vibrant blend of gin, cucumber, tropical fruit, St. Germain, and simple syrup. We then shake it up and pour into chilled martini glasses garnished with fresh mint and cucumber ribbons. We find the cucumber in this sweet and tangy cocktail lends a refreshing twist, evoking images of breezy South American seaside retreats. For the cucumber juice, simply add cucumbers to a blender, blend, and strain the juice. To make the ribbons, remove the outer peel of a cucumber and use a vegetable peeler to peel long, thin strips of the inner flesh.

Makes 4 cocktails

- 1 cup London dry gin
- 1 cup fresh cucumber juice
- ½ cup fresh pineapple juice
- ½ cup fresh lime juice
- ½ cup St. Germain Liqueur
- ¼ cup Simple Syrup (page 2)
- Garnish: Fresh mint sprigs and cucumber ribbons

Fill 4 coupe or martini glasses with ice and set them aside.

Add the gin, cucumber juice, pineapple juice, lime juice, St. Germain, and Simple Syrup to a large cocktail shaker filled with ice. Shake vigorously for 8 seconds. Remove the ice from the chilled glasses and strain the beverage into the glasses. Garnish with fresh mint and cucumber ribbons and serve.

Guayabera

Here's a fantastic cocktail that embodies the flavors of Cuba and the Caribbean. The traditional drink typically consists of rum, guava, lime, and simple syrup, shaken with ice and strained into a glass. At Jaguar, we elevate the tropical flavors with a splash of fresh pineapple juice. The guava purée can be found at grocery stores or online. With its fruity and tangy taste, the Guayabera cocktail is perfect for sipping on a hot summer day, transporting you to a sunny beachside paradise.

Makes 4 cocktails

1 cup Havana Club white rum

1 cup guava purée

½ cup fresh lime juice

½ cup fresh pineapple juice

¼ cup Simple Syrup (page 2)

Garnish: Pineapple fronds, Luxardo cherries, pineapple wedges

Fill 4 rocks or snifter glasses with ice and set aside.

Add the rum, guava purée, lime juice, pineapple juice, and Simple Syrup to a large cocktail shaker filled with ice. Shake vigorously for 8 seconds. Strain in the prepared glasses, garnish, and serve. **Note:** For a more attractive pineapple frond garnish, cut the edges of the frond with a crinkle-cut craft scissor.

Cuban Rum

I've had the pleasure of serving many kinds of Latin American spirits at Jaguar, and Cuban rum is one of those spirits I enjoy. There's a rich history behind it, and every sip tells a story. Cuba's climate and fertile soil create the perfect conditions for growing sugarcane, the main ingredient in rum. The island's rum-making tradition goes back centuries, and it's something they've perfected over generations.

Cuban rum, if you're not familiar, is known for its smoothness and complexity, often featuring notes of vanilla, caramel, and tropical fruit. It's made using the traditional method, which involves aging the rum in oak barrels, where it takes on a deep character and a slight hint of spice. What sets Cuban rum apart is the island's unique climate and the influence of its coastal environment. The salt in the air imparts a subtle maritime quality that you don't find in other rums.

Whether it's part of a classic Mojito, a Cuba Libre, or our delicious Guayabera, Cuban rum offers a perfect balance of sweetness and depth. It's an essential ingredient in many of the cocktails that define Cuba's vibrant culture. So, next time you're enjoying a rum, take a moment to appreciate the craftsmanship and heritage that go into every bottle of Cuban rum.

Michelada Especial

AND MICHELADA CUBANA

The Michelada is a popular Mexican cocktail known for its unique mix of flavors. Typically made with beer, lime juice, assorted sauces, and spices, and served over ice with a salted rim, this spirited drink is perfect for warm-weather gatherings. At Jaguar, we serve our Micheladas tableside with a variety of accoutrements so our guests can customize their Michelada to their liking. For instance, along with Clamato, we offer Maggi Seasoning, Worcestershire, and Tabasco so one can make a Michelada Cubana.

Makes 4 cocktails

RIM
Lime wedges and salt

CUBANO MIXTURE
Makes about 5 cups

3½ cups Maggi Seasoning

1 cup Worcestershire sauce

½ cup Tabasco hot sauce

MICHELADA ESPECIAL
8 ounces fresh lime juice

Clamato juice, as needed, optional

1 or 2 (12-ounce) bottles Mexican beer

Garnish: Lime wedges

Run fresh lime wedges around the rim of 4 pint glasses. Then roll the moistened rims in salt. Fill the glasses with ice, then pour ¼ cup lime juice into each glass. Add a splash of clamato, if desired. Tilt each glass and slowly add the beer until each glass is filled. Gently stir, garnish with lime wedges, and serve with extra beer on the side.

To make the Cubanas, simply omit the Clamato from the ingredient list and add 2 tablespoons of our Cubano Mixture to each glass while refrigerating the extra for the next round—and the rounds after that.

Pisco Sour

The Pisco Sour is a classic cocktail originating from Peru and Chile, each claiming its invention. The drink combines pisco—a grape brandy—with lime juice, simple syrup, egg whites, and Angostura bitters. The drink offers a delightful balance of sweet, sour, and frothy texture. Pisco, the base spirit, provides a unique grape flavor, while the lime juice adds a tangy zest. The egg whites give the cocktail a silky-smooth mouthfeel and a frothy top, which is garnished with drops of Angostura bitters to add a subtle aromatic complexity. The Pisco Sour remains a beloved South American cocktail that's enjoyed nightly by our guests at Jaguar.

Makes 4 cocktails

- 1 cup pisco
- ½ cup Simple Syrup (page 2)
- ½ cup fresh lime juice
- 4 egg whites
- Angostura bitters, as needed
- Garnish: Fresh kaffir lime leaves

Add the pisco, Simple Syrup, lime juice, and egg whites to a large, dry (no ice) cocktail shaker. Shake vigorously for 8 seconds. Add a handful of ice to the shaker and shake vigorously for 10 seconds or until the concoction is foamy. Strain into four rocks glasses, gently add droplets of bitters on top of the foamed surface, garnish, and serve.

Peruvian and Chilean Pisco

As a cocktail aficionado, I have always been fascinated with pisco—not just for its flavor, but for the passionate history behind it. Both Peru and Chile claim pisco as their national spirit, and the rivalry runs deep. Pisco originated in the 16th century when Spanish colonizers brought grapes to South America. They distilled the leftover wine, creating a clear brandy they called "pisco," named after the Peruvian port from which it was exported.

Peruvian and Chilean piscos differ in production. Peruvian pisco is distilled only once, without water added, using copper stills and specific grape varieties. It's strictly regulated, often with a bold, aromatic profile. Chilean pisco, by contrast, is often distilled more than once, is sometimes diluted before bottling, and comes in several styles—from smooth to robust.

Globally, pisco has gained attention for its versatility. The Pisco Sour, a classic drink shaken with lime juice, simple syrup, egg white, and bitters, is a staple in cocktail bars worldwide. Whether Peruvian or Chilean, pisco offers a smooth, grape-forward flavor that shines in both simple and complex drinks. I love introducing customers to its nuances—it's a gateway to South American culture in a glass.

Oscar del

Aceite Merken y Merken Confitado

MERKEN OIL & MERKEN CONFIT

This recipe is very special to me, as it brings me back to my youth and being in the kitchen with my grandmother. She loved slow cooking stews and salsas. I remember the wonderful aromas emanating from her kitchen, which smelled delicious all day long. If you like spicy foods, like I do, this fiery oil is traditionally made with dried chilies and chile de arbol, a small yet potent Mexican chili pepper. Because the pepper can be quite fiery with an aggressive explosion, I adjusted the oil at the restaurant to make it tolerable for our guests yet still capture the essence of its flavors that enhance so many Latin American dishes. Instead of chile de arbol, I use the Merken chili pepper, which is a much milder pepper. The chili, also known as cacho de cabra (goat horn, because of its shape) is traditionally hung over a wood fire to absorb the smoke, which creates the distinctive flavor and color it's known for. If you're looking for a traditional pepper full of flavor without the heat, try the Merken chili pepper.

Makes 4 cups

10 Merken chili peppers (or other desired dried red chili pepper), stems and seeds removed

1 cup red wine vinegar

½ cup soy sauce

1 cup minced garlic

2 cups minced onion

2 cups 80/20 oil blend (80% vegetable oil, 20% olive oil)

Add the peppers to a bowl with the vinegar and soy sauce. Let sit at room temperature overnight. This will allow the peppers to become soft and easy to purée.

Add the softened peppers, vinegar, soy sauce, garlic, onion, and oil to a small saucepan over low heat. Mix well and cook for 1 hour, or until a dark red oily sauce forms. Remove from the heat and let cool. Strain and store in a sealed container until ready to use. **Note:** Reserve what's in the strainer as well. This is the Merken Confit, which we will use in other recipes throughout the book.

Cebolla Morada Encurtida

PICKLED RED ONIONS

Pickling is popular in Latin America. In Mexico, this pickled red onion recipe with its bright pink and purple hues is a classic accompaniment to Cochinita Pibil (Slow-Roasted Pork). I enjoy these refreshing onions because they complement a variety of meats and stews by adding the right balance and crunchy freshness. When you're looking to add a pop of color and flavor to your next meal, make a batch of these delicious pickled onions.

Makes 2 cups

2 large red onions, peeled and sliced thin from top to bottom

2 tablespoons red wine vinegar

½ cup fresh lime juice

2 garlic cloves, peeled and crushed

⅛ teaspoon oregano

1 small piece habanero pepper

1 teaspoon salt

Add the onions, vinegar, lime juice, garlic, oregano, habanero, and salt to a mixing bowl. Mix well until combined. Pour all the contents into a jar, seal, and let rest for at least 2 hours before using.

Chamorritos con Salsa

THREE CHILES GLAZED PORK SHANKS

Here's a fun, unique appetizer we like to serve at Jaguar. The star of this savory bite is a miniature pork shank, which you can easily find and purchase online from Hatfield. The shanks are fully cooked, making these convenient, easy-to-prepare bites ideal for a bar snack, appetizer, or finger food. Once reheated, the tender, mouthwatering pork falls right off the bone, while the bone-in presentation makes them easy to eat. We like to serve them with our homemade Three Chiles Sauce, which is smoky and sweet and pairs well with the pork. As an alternative to mini pork shanks, this recipe also works well with chicken wings and drumettes.

Serves 4

THREE CHILES SAUCE
Makes 2 cups

1 cup grapeseed oil

1 small yellow onion, peeled and finely chopped

1 garlic clove, peeled and minced

1 tablespoon sugar

½ cup water

2 fresh guajillo chiles, cut into thin rings

1 fresh ancho chili, cut into thin rings

3 fresh puya chiles, cut into thin rings

⅓ cup Worcestershire sauce

½ cup apple cider vinegar

PORK SHANKS

8 (5- or 6-ounce) Hatfield Red's Legendary Ribeez Fully Cooked Pork Shanks

½ tablespoon kosher salt

To make the Three Chiles Sauce: Add the oil to a medium-sized saucepot over medium heat. When the oil is hot and shimmering, add the onions and garlic and cook, stirring occasionally, until the onions and garlic are soft, about 5 minutes. Dissolve the sugar in the water and add to the pot. Lower the heat and add the chiles, Worcestershire sauce, and vinegar. Cook, stirring occasionally, for 25 minutes. Remove from heat and set aside until ready to use.

To make the Pork Shanks: Preheat the oven to 300°F. Season the pork shanks with salt and brush the shanks liberally with the Three Chiles Sauce. Place the glazed shanks on a wire rack inside a shallow sheet pan. Roast for 30 minutes, brushing the shanks with additional glaze every 10 minutes. Remove and serve immediately.

Cochinita Pibil

SLOW-ROASTED PORK

This preparation from Yucatán involves a traditional cooking method where you rub the pork parts in achiote and marinate them with sour orange and garlic, wrap them in banana leaves and place them in a hole in the ground full of coals and wood on fire. It takes hours to break down the tissue and absorb all the flavors until you get a magnificent product tested by time. Certainly, the show for me is part of the dish; I enjoy it as much as being in the theater or hearing a friend explaining an intricate concept.

Makes 4 (8-ounce) portions

2 pounds pork shoulder (or butt)

1 tablespoon salt

3 ounces El Yucateco Achiote Paste

1 cup fresh orange juice

¼ cup fresh lime juice

1 banana leaf, cut in half lengthwise, optional

Preheat the oven to 350°F.

Trim the pork and cut into 2-inch cubes. Transfer to a bowl and season with the salt, making sure to rub the salt into the meat. Add the Achiote Paste, orange juice, and lime juice to the bowl and mix well. If you're using the banana leaf, place the 2 banana leaf halves inside a large Pyrex glass dish forming an "X" pattern. Place the pork in the center of the banana leaves or just inside the dish if not using the leaves. Close the ends of the banana leaves on top of the pork and cover the dish tightly with foil. Place in the preheated oven for 3 hours, or until tender and falling apart.

Remove the pork from the oven and let the pork rest for about 30 minutes before removing the foil. When exposed, make sure the pork has cooled. Using a potato masher, crush the large pieces of pork and then use two forks to shred the meat. Reserve any braising liquid to mix in with the pork once it's finished being shredded. Serve in the banana leaves for a dramatic presentation, or transfer the pork to a serving platter and place it alongside toasted buns and assorted condiments such as pickled red onions for mouthwatering pork sliders (page 56).

Pork and Latin America

As a chef deeply inspired by Latin American cuisine, I can tell you that pork has long held a special place in the region's culinary history. Introduced by the Spanish during the colonial era, pigs quickly became a staple due to their adaptability and efficient meat yield. Over time, pork was embraced and reimagined through Indigenous techniques and local ingredients, becoming central to many national dishes.

From the crispy, golden chicharrón of Colombia and Peru to the richly seasoned lechón asado in Cuba and Puerto Rico, pork is not just food—it's part of cultural identity and celebration. In Mexico, carnitas are slow cooked to tender perfection and served in tacos, often during family gatherings and festivals. In Argentina and Brazil, pork features prominently in barbecues, or asados, seasoned simply to let the meat shine.

Pork's popularity endures because of its versatility—it can be braised, roasted, grilled, or fried, and it absorbs bold flavors like citrus, garlic, chili, and spices exceptionally well. Today, chefs across Latin America and beyond continue to innovate with pork, honoring traditional methods while crafting modern interpretations. It remains a beloved protein that connects the past with the present on every plate.

Croquetas de Pescado Ahumado

SMOKED FISH CROQUETTES

Croquetas are one of the most popular snacks or appetizers in Miami. Usually made with smoked ham and a mixture of cream, they are addictive and delicious. At Jaguar, we pay homage to the croqueta by experimenting with different flavors and ingredients. That's how this Smoked Fish Croquette was born. We blend flaky fish with mustard, egg, lime, Parmesan, and sautéed vegetables. Then we coat and deep fry it to golden perfection. The crisp exterior gives way to a tender, flavorful center. We then serve the dish with two vibrant sauces to create a culinary treat that leaves a lasting impression.

Serves 4 (2 croquetas per person)

AJI PANCA SAUCE
Makes 2 cups

3 cloves garlic, peeled

¼ cup red wine vinegar

1 teaspoon cumin

2 tablespoons fresh lime juice

1 white onion, peeled and chopped

¼ cup aji panca paste

¼ cup aji amarillo paste

1 cup 90/10 oil blend (90% vegetable oil, 10% olive oil)

Kosher salt, to taste

AJI AMARILLO AIOLI
Makes 2 cups

4 cloves garlic, peeled and minced

½ cup fresh lime juice

1 teaspoon cumin

½ cup aji amarillo paste

1 cup mayonnaise

SALSA CRIOLLA ROJA
Makes 2 cups

2 red bell peppers, cored, seeded, and thinly sliced

1 red onion, peeled and julienned

1 cup chopped fresh cilantro

½ cup fresh lime juice

1 teaspoon kosher salt

1 tablespoon extra virgin olive oil

OTHER

2 tablespoons unsalted butter

1 medium red onion, peeled and diced

1 cup corn kernels

Kosher or sea salt, as needed

1 pound smoked white fish (see page 35)

1 teaspoon Dijon mustard

3 eggs, divided

2 teaspoons grated Parmesan cheese

1 tablespoon fresh lime juice

1 cup all-purpose flour

1 cup corn flakes

1 cup panko breadcrumbs

4 cups vegetable oil, for frying

To make the Aji Panca Sauce: Add the garlic, vinegar, cumin, lime juice, onion, and both aji pastes to a blender and blend until smooth. Slowly drizzle the oil into the blender in a consistent stream while the blender is running until all the oil has been used. Taste and season with salt and pepper, if necessary. Remove the sauce from the blender and transfer to a squeeze bottle or glass jar until ready to use. The sauce will keep sealed in the refrigerator for up to 5 days.

To make the Aji Amarillo Aioli: Add the garlic, lime juice, cumin, and aji paste to a medium bowl. Mix well until combined. Add the mayonnaise and mix until incorporated. Remove the sauce from the bowl and transfer to a squeeze bottle or glass jar until ready to use. The sauce will keep sealed in the refrigerator for up to 5 days.

To make the Salsa Criolla Roja: Add the peppers, onion, cilantro, lime juice, salt, and oil to a bowl. Mix well, making sure the vegetables are evenly coated. Check and adjust seasoning if necessary. Reserve until ready to use.

Add the butter to a large pot over low heat. When melted, add the onions and corn, and season with a little salt. Sauté the vegetables, stirring occasionally, until the onions are soft, about 5 minutes. Remove from the heat and set aside to cool.

Place the smoked fish, mustard, 1 egg, cheese, lime juice, and the cooled onions and corn in a bowl. Mix gently but well. Refrigerate for about 30 minutes, which will help firm up the mixture.

Add the oil to a large Dutch oven or pot over medium-high heat. Heat the oil to 325°F. Use a candy or digital thermometer to check the temperature. **Note:** You may need to reduce your heat if the oil gets above 325°F.

Set up a breading station by adding the flour to a shallow dish. Beat the two remaining eggs and place them in another shallow dish beside the flour. Then combine the corn flakes and breadcrumbs and add them to a third shallow dish next to the eggs.

Remove the fish mixture from the refrigerator and form the mixture into small, golf ball–sized balls. Then dip each ball, first in the flour, then the eggs, and finally in the corn flake-breadcrumb mixture, ensuring the entire ball is breaded.

Carefully place the croquetas in the hot oil and deep fry until golden brown and crispy, about 3 minutes. **Note:** If you don't intend to fry the croquetas right away, you can store them in a sealed container (without stacking or overcrowding) in the refrigerator, up to 4 days. To help achieve a uniform golden-brown color, use a long-slotted spoon or a spiral wire skimmer to help move the balls around. Carefully remove the croquetas from the oil and place on a large plate lined with paper towels to drain. Season with salt.

To serve, add 2 tablespoons of the Aji Panca Sauce and 2 tablespoons of the Aji Amarillo Aioli each to 4 serving plates. Top with two croquetas per plate. Garnish with the Salsa Criolla Roja and serve.

Smoked White Fish

When I'm talking about smoked white fish, I'm referring to a variety of fish that are smoked after being cleaned, filleted, and brined. Common species include cod, corvina, and halibut. The smoking process involves exposing the fish to smoke from burning wood chips, which imparts a distinct smoky flavor while preserving the fish. Smoked white fish is versatile and can be enjoyed on its own as a delicacy or used as an ingredient in various dishes like our Croquetas. The fish's white flaky texture and rich, savory taste make it a popular choice for seafood lovers seeking a flavorful and satisfying culinary experience. You can find smoked white fish at many seafood markets that sell smoked fish.

Empanadas de Verde

PLANTAIN PATTIES EMPANADA

Empanadas are a popular dish in Latin America, consisting of a pastry filled with various ingredients, then baked or fried. The fillings vary by region and can incude meats like beef or chicken, vegetables, cheese, or even sweet options like fruit. Because empanadas are versatile, we like to serve them as an appetizer or snack, which also make them the perfect bite for family gatherings and celebrations. This recipe features green (unripe) plantains, which we use in both the dough and filling. If you haven't worked with unripe plantains, you'll find they can be difficult to peel. I like to cut a long slit lengthwise in the peel, just deep enough to penerate the flesh. Then I'll soak the plantain in hot water for several minutes. This will help to loosen the skin and make them easier to peel. Try these delicious empanadas at your next gathering. The result is a delightful combination of a crisp crust and a flavor that's mildly earthy and slightly sweet thanks to the green plantain.

Serves 4

EMPANADA DOUGH
4 green plantains, peeled and sliced into 6 to 8 rounds

1 teaspoon kosher salt

1 large egg

2 tablespoons unsalted butter

4 cups oil, for frying

CHEESE FILLING
1 cup queso fresco cheese

1 cup mozzarella

½ cup green onions, both green and white parts, finely chopped

GARNISH
Sea salt

Pickled Slaw, page 128

Pickled Red Onions, page 24

Fill a medium-sized saucepot with water and bring to a boil over high heat. Add the plantains and salt and boil for 30 minutes, or until tender. Remove and drain. Grate the number of pieces that make up 1 plantain (about 6 to 8 rounds) in a large bowl and place the remaining pieces from the other 3 plantains into a food processor. Add the egg and butter to the food processor and mix until combined. Transfer the mixture to the bowl with the grated plantain and mix well. Form 8 small (golf ball–size) balls and then gently flatten with a rolling pin. Set aside.

Make the Cheese Filling by adding the two cheeses and green onions to a mixing bowl. Mix well until combined.

Add 2 to 3 tablespoons of the cheese mixture to each rolled-out dough, then fold the dough over the filling and crimp the edges of the dough closed using your fingers or a fork. Refrigerate for 15 minutes to 1 hour for the empanadas to set.

Add the oil to a stockpot over medium-high heat. Heat the oil until the temperature reaches 350°F. Use a candy thermometer to monitor the temperature. When the oil is at temperature, carefully add the empanadas one at a time and fry in batches to avoid overcrowding and the temperature of the oil dropping too rapidly. Fry until golden brown and crispy, about 2 minutes. Remove the empanadas and drain on a paper towel–lined plate. Repeat with the remaining empanadas. Serve hot with a sprinkling of sea salt, Pickled Slaw, and Pickled Red Onions.

Plantains

I've always been fascinated by the versatility and cultural significance of plantains. Native to Southeast Asia, plantains made their way across continents through trade routes, eventually becoming a staple in African, Caribbean, Latin American, and Southeast Asian cuisines. Unlike their sweeter cousin, the banana, plantains are starchier and more adaptable to both savory and sweet preparations, depending on their ripeness.

Across the Caribbean and Latin America, you'll find them as tostones or maduros—fried green or ripe slices, respectively. Their ability to complement spices, meats, and sauces has made them indispensable in home kitchens and fine dining alike.

Today, plantains are gaining popularity worldwide, especially among those seeking gluten-free, whole-food alternatives. Their nutritional value—being rich in fiber, potassium, and vitamins—also contributes to their appeal. I love using plantains because they offer a comforting texture, absorb flavor beautifully, and evoke a sense of tradition. Whether crisped into chips, roasted, or puréed into a creamy base, plantains connect modern plates with centuries of culinary heritage. Their global journey continues, and their role in contemporary cooking is only expanding.

Guacamole

I don't know anyone who doesn't love freshly made guacamole—that zesty classic I like to refer to as "green gold." I remember visiting my grandparents' house on Sundays when I was a young boy. They lived in a charming little pueblo called Ojo de Agua just outside Mexico City. They always had a feast ready for us, nothing fancy, but an endless array of delicious food—and plenty of tequila and wine for the adults. I vividly recall the crispy chicharrons (pork rinds) that they served with their guacamole, which was mashed to perfection. They were full of flavor and offered the perfect crunch paired with the creaminess of the guacamole. At Jaguar, we serve our guacamole with crispy pork rinds and tortilla chips. We also spread our guacamole on our Chicken Bacon Sandwich for an extra layer of tangy goodness.

Makes 4 cups

10 ripe avocados

2 tablespoons fresh lime juice

½ jalapeño, diced (remove seeds to reduce heat level, if desired)

½ white onion, peeled and diced

1 bunch fresh cilantro, finely chopped

1 tablespoon kosher salt, or to taste

Cut the avocados in half, going from pole to pole around the pit. Gently twist the avocado to separate the halves. Remove the pit then scoop out the flesh and add to a large bowl. **Note:** The avocado flesh will turn brown quickly so work relatively fast. Add to the bowl the lime juice, jalapeño, onion, cilantro, and salt. Mash the avocados with the ingredients until you achieve the consistency you like. At the restaurant, we prefer a smooth guacamole as opposed to chunky. Taste and adjust the seasoning if needed. Serve immediately.

Jibarito

PLANTAIN & STEAK SANDWICH

The jibarito is a Puerto Rican sandwich that substitutes bread with flattened, fried green plantains. Originating in Chicago's Puerto Rican community, it's typically filled with thinly sliced steak, lettuce, tomato, cheese, and some sort of garlic mayonnaise. At Jaguar, we make the mouthwatering sandwich featuring our juicy Braised Brisket and zesty Chipotle Aioli.

Serves 4 (1 small sandwich each)

BRAISED BRISKET
Serves 6 to 8

- ½ cup vegetable oil
- 1 (2-pound) trimmed brisket, cut into 2 to 4 pieces for easier handling
- 2 tablespoons kosher salt
- 1 white onion, peeled and roughly chopped
- ½ medium carrot, roughly chopped
- ½ red bell pepper, roughly chopped
- 2 cloves garlic, peeled and roughly chopped
- 1 pound tomatoes, roughly chopped
- 1 bay leaf
- 1 teaspoon dried cumin
- 1 tablespoon paprika
- 4 cups water
- ½ cup apple cider vinegar
- 1 cup orange juice

CHIPOTLE AIOLI
Makes about 1 cup

- 2 cloves garlic, peeled
- 1 tablespoon fresh lime juice
- 1 teaspoon chipotle in adobo sauce
- 1 cup mayonnaise
- ⅛ teaspoon salt

OTHER

- ¼ cup vegetable oil, for frying
- 4 green plantains, peeled
- 8 slices Braised Brisket
- 4 slices American cheese
- 4 tomato slices
- 4 romaine lettuce leaves
- 4 thick slices (¼-inch) red onion
- ¼ cup Chipotle Aioli

To make the Braised Brisket: Preheat the oven to 350°F. Heat a large heavy pot over high heat, add the oil, and heat until shimmering. Season the brisket pieces with salt and sear until deeply browned on all sides. Remove the brisket from the pot and set aside. Add the onion, carrot, bell pepper, garlic, and tomatoes to the same pot and reduce the heat to medium heat. Cook until the vegetables are softened and golden. Stir in the bay leaf, cumin, and paprika. Add the water, vinegar, and orange juice, and bring to a boil. Remove from the heat and return the brisket pieces to the pot, distributing them evenly. Cover with a lid and braise in the oven for 4 hours, or until the meat is fork tender. Let the meat cool to room temperature in the brisket braising liquid. Once cooled, remove the brisket and store separately. Finally, transfer the vegetables and braising liquid to a blender and purée until smooth. Season to taste with salt. Store the sauce in containers for later use or return to the brisket to keep the meat moist and flavorful.

To make the Chipotle Aioli: Add the garlic, lime juice, and chipotle to a blender or use a handheld immersion blender. Blend until smooth. Add the mayonnaise and blend again with a spatula until fully incorporated and creamy. Season with salt.

To make the Jibarito: Add the oil to a large skillet over medium-high heat.

While the oil is heating, cut each peeled plantain in half lengthwise, yielding 4 halves. Add one plantain half and fry for about 1 minute on both sides. Remove and drain on a paper towel-lined plate. Cover each plantain half with a sheet of plastic wrap, then using a bacon press, slowly press down on the half, gently crushing the plantain until it's as thin as possible, about ¼ inch. Repeat with the remaining 3 plantain pieces. Set aside.

Wipe out the oil from the skillet and place over medium heat. Add the brisket slices and top with the cheese. Cook until the brisket is hot, and the cheese is melted. Remove from the heat and set aside.

Arrange 4 of the pressed plantains halves on a platter or 4 individual serving plates. Spread the plantains with the Chipotle Aioli, reserving half of the Aioli for the tops. Divide the brisket and cheese evenly and place on top of the Chipotle Aioli–covered plantain. Place the tomato slices, lettuce, and onion on top of the meat and cheese. Spread the remaining Chipotle Aioli on the top of the remaining plantain, place on top of the onion, and serve.

Puerto Rico's Beloved Sandwich

Though deeply associated with Puerto Rican culture, the jibarito originated in Chicago in 1996, created by Juan "Peter" Figueroa at Borinquen Restaurant in the city's Humboldt Park neighborhood, a historically Puerto Rican community. The name jibarito means "little jíbaro," referencing the rural peasant farmers who symbolize Puerto Rican cultural pride and simplicity.

While not native to Puerto Rico, the jibarito was embraced on the island and quickly became popular due to its distinct blend of familiar flavors. It typically features steak, garlic mayo, lettuce, tomato, and cheese layered between crisp plantain slices, offering a savory and satisfying alternative to traditional sandwiches.

Its popularity in Puerto Rico grew in the early 2000s as local chefs and street vendors adapted the dish, adding their own regional twists. Today, it can be found across the island at food trucks, restaurants, and even in home kitchens. The jibarito stands as a cultural bridge—originating in the diaspora, celebrated on the island—highlighting the global nature of Puerto Rican identity and culinary innovation.

Pure de Frijol

BLACK BEANS & PURÉE

Beans are a staple in Latin America and were quite common in my home growing up. My grandma from my mother's side was an exceptional cook and she'd prepare beans in enormous quantities. She taught me that cooking beans is a two-part process. The first part is to clean the beans. I always believed this was an excuse for my mom and grandma to sit around the kitchen table, while we kids were at school, so they could gossip. The second part is using the pressure cooker. I vividly remember coming home from school and being enveloped by the sounds of the pressure cooker working its magic and the enticing aromas within. I find black beans are magic. In this recipe, we use them as a purée, but they're also fantastic in our Black Bean Soup (page 148).

Makes 2 cups

½ pound dried black beans, rinsed and cleaned

4 cups water

1 small onion, peeled and finely chopped

½ bunch fresh cilantro, tied with butcher twine

1 tablespoon olive oil

1 teaspoon salt

Add the beans, water, onion, cilantro, olive oil, and salt, then set an Instant Pot to "Pressure Cook" and cook on high for 30 minutes. Keep in mind it takes about 8 minutes for the pot to fully pressurize before the timer begins. Once the cooking cycle ends, let the beans rest in the pot for another 20 minutes so the steam releases naturally—don't touch any buttons. I always set a timer here so I remember when it's safe to open the lid.

When you lift the lid, the beans should be tender and deeply flavorful. If not, it usually means the beans were a little old or the water a bit hard. In that case, reseal and cook on high for another 10 to 20 minutes. Keep warm until ready to serve. You can also refrigerate the beans in an airtight container up to 5 days, or 1 month in the freezer.

For a silky Black Bean Purée, blend the beans directly in the pot using an immersion blender, until smooth, adding a splash of water if needed.

Queso Fundido

MELTED CHEESE

If you haven't tried our Queso Fundido, you must. That's, of course, if you enjoy a mouthwatering delight of irresistible cheese. The melted blend of manchego, Gouda, and mozzarella pairs perfectly with our Sautéed Poblano Pepper Mix, creating a bold, savory flavor in every bite. Scooped up with warm tortillas or crispy chips, it's the ultimate comfort food. The stretchy, molten texture and smoky, seasoned taste make it impossible to resist. One bite, and you'll be hooked on this decadent, soul-satisfying Jaguar favorite.

Serves 4

3 CHEESE BLEND
Makes about 8 cups

½ pound shredded aged manchego

½ pound shredded Gouda

1 pound shredded mozzarella

SAUTÉED POBLANO PEPPER MIX
Makes 2 cups

½ cup vegetable oil

3 cups red onion, peeled and cut into strips lengthwise

1 cup poblano peppers, cut into strips

1 cup fresh corn kernels

1 teaspoon salt

PICO DE GALLO
Makes 2 cups

2 cups diced tomato

1 tablespoon diced jalapeño

¼ cup fresh lime juice

¼ cup extra virgin olive oil

1 cup chopped fresh cilantro

1 cup diced red onion

1 teaspoon kosher salt

12 (6-inch) flour tortillas, warmed

To make the 3 Cheese Blend: Add the manchego, Gouda, and mozzarella to a bowl and gently mix until blended. Store in a sealed plastic bag in the refrigerator until needed.

To make the Sautéed Poblano Pepper Mix: Add the oil to a large cast-iron skillet over high heat. When the oil is hot, add the onion, peppers, corn, and salt. Stir to combine and let cook. The high heat will char the vegetables while softening them. Stir often to get equal char on all the vegetables. When the vegetables are softened and well charred, about 5 minutes, remove them from the pan and set them aside until ready to use. **Note:** Don't worry if the vegetables are a little crunchy. They will soften more when they get broiled with the 3 Cheese Blend.

To make the Pico de Gallo: Add the tomato,

jalapeño, lime juice, oil, cilantro, onion, and salt to a bowl. Mix well until combined. Set aside until ready to use. If not using immediately, store in a sealed container in the refrigerator for up to 3 or 4 days.

Preheat the oven to broil and move one of the shelves just under the heating element.

Add the 3 Cheese Blend to a cold cast-iron skillet. Add the Sautéed Poblano on top. Place the skillet in the preheated oven and broil until the cheese has melted evenly and is nice and brown, about 10 minutes. Carefully remove from the oven and set the hot skillet on a large wood cutting board. Serve with warm tortillas and Pico de Gallo.

Quesadilla de Tres Quesos

THREE CHEESE QUESADILLA

The quesadilla is a beloved Mexican dish that is in a class of its own, as there are infinite possibilities and fillings. Most feature a tortilla filled with melted cheese and accompanied by meats, vegetables, or beans. Grilled to perfection, the quesadilla delivers a satisfying crunch on the outside and a warm, comforting center. Its versatility makes the quesadilla a favorite for any meal or occasion. At Jaguar, our quesadilla features a high-quality flour tortilla that is durable enough to hold the gooey filling inside. The quesadilla is truly perfection.

Makes 4 (10-inch) quesadillas

4 (10-inch) flour tortillas

4 cups 3 Cheese Blend (page 50)

1 cup Sautéed Poblano Pepper Mix (page 50)

½ cup Merken Oil (page 22)

½ cup chopped fresh curly parsley

2 cups Guacamole (page 40)

1 cup Pico de Gallo (page 50)

1 cup sour cream

Set the tortillas flat on a kitchen counter or flat surface. Divide the cheese blend evenly and add to half of each tortilla. Top the cheese with an even amount of Sautéed Poblano Pepper Mix. Fold the other side of the tortillas to close.

Add the Merken Oil and parsley to a large cast-iron skillet or pan over medium heat. When the oil is heated, add the tortillas. **Note:** You will likely need to cook in batches to not overcrowd the pan. Sear until the tortilla is toasted to a nice golden brown and the cheese is melted. Gently turn the tortillas over and repeat on the other side. Remove the tortillas from the pan and transfer to a cutting board. Cut each tortilla in 4 pieces. Serve with a side of Guacamole, Pico de Gallo, and sour cream.

Sandwich de Cochinita con Pure de Frijol y Cebolla Morada Encurtida

PULLED PORK SLIDERS WITH BLACK BEAN PURÉE & PICKLED RED ONIONS

These sliders are all about our slow-roasted pork. Marinated in achiote, orange juice, and spices, the seasoned pork is wrapped in banana leaves and cooked slowly for added flavor and moisture. This recipe is a traditional Mexican dish originating from the Yucatán and makes a wonderful finger food. Some of our regular bar guests ask us not to toast their bun so the soft bread has an easier time soaking up the braising liquid from the pork. In their words, "It's pure culinary gold!" Whether toasted or not, these mouthwatering sliders are a hit. Feel free to increase the recipe. At home, I will make at least 4 sliders per person and serve them with ice-cold cervezas, but that's just me.

Serves 4 (one slider per person)

- 4 slider buns, toasted
- ¼ cup Black Bean Purée (page 48)
- 1 cup Cochinita Pibil (page 28)
- ¼ cup Pickled Red Onions (page 24)
- 1 bunch fresh watercress, stems removed

Place the bottom of the toasted slider buns on a serving platter or wood serving board. Spread the Black Bean Purée evenly on the buns and then mound ¼ cup of the Cochinita on top of the beans. Arrange the Pickled Red Onions and watercress on top, finish with the top bun, and serve.

Tostada de Ceviche

CEVICHE TOSTADAS

Enjoy these mouthwatering ceviche tostadas, which are a blend of zesty, fresh flavors and satisfying crunch. Our citrus-marinated seafood is served atop a crisp tostada shell accompanied by our Aji Amarillio Aioli, Coleslaw, and legendary Salsa Muerte. This dish is not only delicious but light and refreshing—perfect for warm weather. Originating from coastal Latin America, ceviche is believed to date back over 2,000 years, with Peru often credited as its birthplace.

Serves 4

COLESLAW
Makes 3½ cups

2 cups shredded Napa cabbage

½ cup shredded carrot

½ cup thinly sliced red onion

½ cup thinly sliced red bell pepper

½ teaspoon crushed caraway seeds

1 cup roughly chopped fresh cilantro

1 teaspoon kosher salt

½ teaspoon fresh cracked black pepper

CEVICHE TOSTADAS

8 tostadas

4 tablespoons Aji Amarillo Aioli (page 32)

4 cups Ceviche Peruano (page 167)

1 cup Coleslaw

Salsa Muerte (page 210)

To make the Coleslaw: Add the cabbage, carrot, onion, bell pepper, caraway seeds, cilantro, salt, and pepper to a large bowl. Mix well to combine, and refrigerate, covered, until ready to use.

To make the Ceviche Tostadas: Place 2 tostadas on each individual serving plate. Spread ½ tablespoon Aji Amarillio Aioli on each tostada. Divide the Coleslaw evenly amongst the tostadas. **Note:** Don't add too much Coleslaw, just a little bed to hold the ceviche. Add ½ cup ceviche to each tostada. Top with a couple of drops of Salsa Muerte (or your favorite salsa) and serve.

Tostones Bacalao Belinda

CRISPY TOSTONES TOPPED WITH CODFISH STEW

Tostones Bacalao Belinda is a delightful Caribbean dish that combines crispy fried plantains with a savory codfish stew. The tostones, made from unripe green plantains, are sliced and fried until golden and crisp. This process creates a crunchy base that perfectly complements the rich, flavorful codfish stew.

The cod, which we soak overnight, is cooked with a medley of ingredients including onions, garlic, tomatoes, and bell peppers. The addition of pepperoncini adds depth to the dish, creating a robust and aromatic stew that enhances the mild taste of the plantains. The combination of the crispy tostones and the soft, flavorful bacalao is irresistible.

This dish, a blend of texture and taste that's often served at Jaguar, is a popular appetizer in Caribbean cuisine, particularly in Puerto Rico and the Dominican Republic. Enjoy this dish at home, where it is sure to be a crowd-pleasing and satisfying meal.

Serves 4

CODFISH STEW

2 pounds salted cod

1 cup olive oil

8 cloves garlic, divided (4 crushed, 4 finely chopped)

3 white onions, chopped small

1 cup tomato paste

6 fresh tomatoes, seeded and chopped

2 cups chopped roasted and peeled red bell pepper, divided

3 cups chopped fresh Italian flat-leaf parsley, divided, plus more for garnish

4 cups creamer or other baby potatoes

1 cup toasted almonds, plus more for garnish

½ cup golden raisins

1½ cups pimento-stuffed olives

1 cup sliced pepperoncini, plus more for garnish

TOSTONES

2 green plantains, peeled and thinly sliced on the bias

4 cups oil, for frying

Kosher salt, to taste

Add the cod to a large bowl and fill with 3 quarts cold water to desalinize the fish. Refrigerate overnight.

Remove the cod from the water and reserve the water for later use. Shred the cod by hand, cleaning and removing any hard pieces and bones. Shred the meat into small pieces and reserve in the refrigerator until ready to use.

Add the oil to a large saucepot over medium heat. When shimmering, add the 4 cloves crushed garlic and sauté, stirring occasionally, until the garlic is dark golden brown, but not burnt, about 10 minutes. Remove the garlic and discard (or save for another use). Add the onions to the garlic-infused oil and cook, stirring occasionally, until the onions are soft and translucent, 7 to 10 minutes. Add the remaining 4 cloves chopped garlic and cook, stirring often, until the garlic is soft and lightly golden, about 5 minutes. Add the tomato paste and tomatoes and stir with a wooden spoon until combined. Add 1 cup of the chopped roasted peppers along with ½ cup of the codfish water. Mix to combine and continue to cook for 10 minutes. Add the remaining cup of roasted peppers and 2 cups of parsley and stir to combine. Cook for 2 minutes, then stir in the shredded cod. Cook for 5 minutes. Stir in the potatoes, almonds, raisins, and olives. Cover and simmer for 30 minutes. Uncover, turn off the heat, and stir in the remaining cup of parsley along with the pepperoncini. Let rest for 30 minutes.

While the Codfish Stew is resting, make the Tostones.

Add enough oil to cover the bottom of a large skillet by ½ inch. Heat over medium-high heat until shimmering. Add the sliced plantain and fry on both sides until golden brown, about 5 minutes per side. Remove and drain on a plate lined with paper towels. Season with salt.

Arrange the fried Tostones on a serving platter and top with the Codfish Stew. Garnish with crushed almonds, chopped parsley, and pepperoncini rings, and serve.

What Is Salted Cod?

Salted cod, or bacalao, holds a revered place in the Latin American culinary tradition, tracing its roots to the colonial era. As a chef, I see it not just as an ingredient, but as a symbol of cultural fusion and resilience. Introduced by European traders, particularly the Portuguese and Spanish, salted cod was ideal for long ocean voyages—its preservation through salt meant it could endure tropical climates without refrigeration. It quickly became a staple throughout the Caribbean, Central America, and the Andes, particularly during Catholic Lent when meat was forbidden.

Through the generations, each country made bacalao its own. In the Dominican Republic, it's enjoyed in stews with tomatoes and peppers. In Puerto Rico, it's served as crispy bacalaítos fritters. Mexicans savor it in bacalao a la Vizcaína, a dish inherited from Basque settlers. Its versatility is unmatched—soaking and rehydrating the fish transforms it, allowing flavors to develop deeply in a variety of dishes.

Even today, bacalao remains popular, especially during religious and national holidays. For me, it represents how necessity and creativity blend in the kitchen, producing dishes that honor both ancestry and adaptability. It's not just food—it's a story preserved in salt, passed down on every plate.

Yucas con Mojo y Aji Amarillo Aioli

CRISPY YUCA WITH SOUR ORANGE CUBAN MOJO & AJI AMARILLO AIOLI

If you're ready for a delicious twist on the classic french fry, you must try these tasty yuca sticks. They're a crispy, golden delight, offering a crunchy exterior that gives way to a soft, starchy center that's rich and satisfying. Like fries, they pair perfectly with dipping sauces like our Sour Orange Cuban Mojo and Aji Amarillo Aioli, but their subtle nuttiness and hearty texture make them uniquely flavorful. Fried to perfection, yuca sticks deliver a comforting bite that's both familiar and exotic, making them an irresistible alternative to traditional potato fries.

Serves 4

- 2 pounds fresh yuca (or substitute with frozen or canned; see next page)
- Kosher salt, for seasoning
- Canola oil, for frying
- 1 cup Sour Orange Cuban Mojo (page 220)
- 1 cup Aji Amarillo Aioli (page 32)

To prepare fresh yuca: Remove the outer layer of the yuca root, which is strong, waxy and typically dark brown, with a vegetable peeler or knife. Next, cut and remove both ends of the root. Slice the root in half lengthwise and remove the center stem. The stem is hard and will not soften even when cooked. Next, slice the root into sticks. Boil the sticks in salted water for 4 minutes, remove, and pat dry with paper towels. Fry the yuca in vegetable oil (heated to 350°F) like you would french fries, turning occasionally, until golden brown and crispy on all sides. Remove, drain, and season with salt. Serve immediately with the Sour Orange Cuban Mojo poured over the top and the Aji Amarillo Aioli on the side as a dipping sauce.

Other Yuca Options

Canned

Since canned yuca is already cooked, simply remove the center stem and slice the yuca into sticks. **Note:** Work with caution since canned yuca is relatively soft. Drain the sticks and dry with paper towels. Fry as noted above until golden brown and crispy, 7 to 9 minutes per side, then prepare and serve in the same manner as the fresh yuca.

Frozen

Frozen yuca is often available whole or in pieces. Thaw the yuca in the refrigerator overnight, then follow the same directions for fresh yuca.

THE MORNING MEAL

As the chef and owner of Jaguar, I like to bring the vibrant flavors of Latin America to life through a masterful preparation of traditional breakfast dishes. I find each plate is a celebration of regional culture, rich heritage, and bold ingredients. From Venezuelan Cachapas, pancakes made from fresh corn batter, and Mexico's Chilaquiles that are lightly fried and simmered in red salsa until tender, to a hearty beef sandwich from Uruguay, we like to capture the essence of morning meals across the continent. At Jaguar, our kitchen becomes a journey through flavor, where tropical fruits, aromatic spices, and rustic techniques take center stage. Whether it's a traditional Yucatán breakfast or Mexico's famous Huevos Rancheros, every dish tells a story of community and tradition. With passion and precision, we enjoy transforming simple ingredients into unforgettable experiences, inviting our guests to start their day with authenticity and soul. Latin America's mornings have never tasted more delicious.

Cachapas

SAVORY-SWEET CORN PANCAKES

Cachapa is a traditional Venezuelan dish made from fresh corn batter, similar to a pancake. Cooked on a griddle, the cakes have a slightly sweet and savory flavor. We like to top them with fresh banana, hickory-smoked bacon, powdered sugar, and maple syrup for an indulgent morning treat. Originating from rural areas, cachapas are popular street food, enjoyed for their rich, comforting taste.

Serves 4
(or about 12 cakes)

CACHAPA

3 cups fresh corn kernels (removed from cob)

3 large eggs

2 cups whole milk

2 tablespoons granulated sugar

1 teaspoon kosher salt

2 tablespoons unsalted butter, plus more for cooking

1 teaspoon pure vanilla extract

1 teaspoon baking powder

⅔ cup Maseca masa harina

OTHER

8 Cachapa

2 ripe bananas, sliced

8 slices cooked hickory smoked bacon

½ cup powdered sugar

1 cup pure maple syrup

To make the Cachapa batter: Add the corn, eggs, milk, sugar, salt, butter, vanilla, baking powder, and Maseca masa harina to a blender and blend until smooth. Next, add a little butter to a large cast-iron skillet or pan over medium heat. When the butter is melted, ladle about ½ cup of the batter in the buttered skillet or pan. Cook for 1½ to 2 minutes, then flip and cook the other side until cooked through. Remove from the heat and keep warm until ready to serve.

To assemble: Place two or three Cachapa on each plate. Arrange the bananas on top. Top with the bacon, powdered sugar, maple syrup, and serve.

Chilaquiles Rojos

FRIED CORN TORTILLAS WITH RED SALSA

Mexicans love their chilaquiles, and this recipe stems from my childhood and the chilaquiles my mother used to make for me. This traditional dish features lightly fried corn tortillas cut into quarters and simmered in red salsa until tender. The chilaquiles are then topped with red onion, cheese, crema, fresh cilantro, and a fried egg. Served with a side of black beans, this flavorful and hearty dish is the perfect breakfast or brunch item, providing a wonderful blend of textures and a savory, slightly tangy taste.

Serves 4

SALSA RANCHERA
Makes about 4 cups

½ cup vegetable oil

1 white onion, peeled and roughly chopped

3 cloves garlic, peeled and roughly chopped

2 dried guajillo chiles, stems and seeds removed

2 pounds fresh tomatoes, roughly chopped

1 jalapeño, stem removed

1 tablespoon kosher salt

1 cup fresh cilantro

BRUNCH CREMA
Makes 2 cups

1 cup heavy cream

1 cup sour cream

CHILAQUILES ROJOS

4 cups corn oil

8 (6-inch) corn tortillas, cut into bite-sized triangles

Kosher salt, as needed

2 tablespoons Merken Oil (page 22)

4 large eggs

6 cups Salsa Ranchera, heated

1 cup thinly sliced red onion

2 cups Panela cheese

2 cups Brunch Crema

¼ cup finely chopped fresh cilantro

4 cups Black Beans (page 48)

To make the Salsa Ranchera: Add the oil to a stockpot or Dutch oven over medium heat. When the oil is shimmering, add the onions and cook for about 5 minutes, then stir in the garlic. Add the guajillo chiles and cook for 2 minutes, until they turn bright red. Add the tomatoes and jalapeño and cook on medium heat for 25 minutes, stirring occasionally.

Transfer the mixture to a blender and carefully purée until smooth, using caution with hot liquids. (For safety, you can allow the mixture to cool slightly before blending, then reheat when ready to use.) Stir in the salt and finish with the cilantro. The salsa can be served warm straight from the pot or cooled and stored in the refrigerator, then reheated as needed.

To make the Brunch Crema: Add the heavy cream and sour cream to a large bowl and whisk until combined. Refrigerate until ready to use.

To make the Chilaquiles Rojos: Add the oil to a Dutch oven over medium-high heat until the temperature registers 350°F. Use a candy or digital thermometer to check the temperature. When the oil is at temperature, add the tortillas. Use a slotted spoon or spider strainer to move the tortillas so they fry evenly. Continue to cook for 3 to 4 minutes, or until they're golden in color. Remove the tortillas and transfer to a paper towel–lined plate to drain. Season with salt.

Add the Merken Oil to a large skillet over medium heat. When the oil is heated, add the eggs and fry sunny side up. Remove from the heat and set aside.

Add the tortilla chips to a large bowl and drizzle with the warm Salsa Ranchera to coat the chips without breaking them. Gently remove and transfer to 4 individual serving bowls. Top with the red onion and Panela cheese, and garnish with the Brunch Crema and cilantro. Place the eggs on top and serve with a side of Black Beans.

More about Chilaquiles

Being from Mexico, naturally I have a deep respect for traditional Mexican cuisine. That's why I find chilaquiles a beautiful example of resourcefulness and flavor. This dish dates back to the Aztec era, where day-old tortillas were repurposed to avoid waste. Over time, the recipe evolved, incorporating ingredients like salsa, cheese, crema, and eggs or shredded chicken, reflecting the diversity of regional Mexican cooking.

As I mentioned in the recipe, chilaquiles are made by lightly frying tortilla pieces, then simmering them in red or green salsa until they're perfectly tender but still hold texture. The dish is then garnished with a variety of toppings—each cook and region adding their own twist. It's a staple breakfast in many Mexican households and often enjoyed as a comforting cure for a late night.

Today, chilaquiles have gained international popularity, appearing on brunch menus around the world. Their balance of crispy, saucy, spicy, and creamy elements is irresistible. As a chef, I love making chilaquiles because they celebrate humble ingredients with bold flavor and tell a story of tradition, adaptability, and culinary creativity.

Chivito Uruguayo

BEEF SANDWICH FROM URUGUAY

Your mouth will need a workout to get it around this enormous breakfast sandwich that's loaded with plenty of flavors and textures and fit for a large appetite. If you'd like to "shrink" the size a bit, gently press the sandwich with a bacon press until it compresses and the egg yolks start to run.

Serves 4

- 4 hamburger buns, toasted
- Vegetable oil, as needed
- ½ pound Braised Brisket (page 42)
- 4 slices Gouda cheese
- ¼ cup Aji Amarillo Aioli (page 32)
- 4 romaine lettuce leaves
- 4 thinly sliced red onion rings
- 4 slices tomato
- Kosher salt, as needed
- 4 pieces (2 x 3 inches) red bell pepper
- 8 slices cooked hickory-smoked bacon
- 4 teaspoons Chimichurri (page 110)
- 4 large eggs

Plate the toasted buns on individual serving plates and set aside.

Add some oil to a large skillet over medium-high heat. When the oil is heated, add the brisket and form into 4 circular "patties." Add the cheese and let it melt slightly.

While the cheese is melting, spread the Aji Amarillo Aioli on each toasted bun bottom. Add the lettuce to each bun, followed by the onion and tomato. Season the top of each tomato with a little salt.

Add the bell pepper and cooked bacon to the skillet and cook until the peppers have softened, 2 to 3 minutes. Place each piece of pepper on top of the brisket and cheese patties and cook for another 2 minutes. Remove each patty from the skillet and place on top of the tomatoes, followed by the bacon and Chimichurri.

Add the eggs to the skillet with a little more oil, if necessary, and fry sunny side up. Remove from the skillet and add to the top and finish by adding the top bun. Use an appetizer toothpick to hold it all together and serve.

Uruguay and Its Beef

As you well know by now, I have a deep appreciation for Latin American cuisine. That's why I can confidently say that Uruguayan beef holds a special place in the culinary world. Uruguay is known for its pristine pastures and free-range cattle, which produce beef that is exceptionally tender, flavorful, and rich in nutrients. The country's commitment to natural grazing methods and minimal use of antibiotics or hormones ensures a high-quality product that chefs like me love to work with.

In Latin America, beef is not just food—it's culture. From the asado traditions of Uruguay and Argentina to the hearty stews of Brazil and Colombia, beef is at the heart of countless beloved dishes. What sets Uruguayan beef apart is its consistency and taste. Whether grilled over open flames or slow cooked in traditional recipes like our brisket for the beef sandwich, its natural marbling and deep flavor shine through.

Uruguayan beef has gained popularity across Latin America due to its premium quality and the country's strong export reputation. As demand grows for authentic, grass-fed meats, more chefs and home cooks alike are turning to Uruguay's offerings. For us in the kitchen, it's a reliable, flavorful foundation that elevates any dish—from a simple steak to a complex, regional specialty.

Desayuno Yucatán
YUCATÁN BREAKFAST

A traditional Yucatán breakfast often includes slow-roasted pork marinated in achiote and citrus and served with warm tortillas. At Jaguar, we like to build upon the delicious blend of flavors and textures unique to the region by adding fried eggs and our homemade Pickled Red Onions. We serve this hearty dish with a side of our homemade Guacamole and invite our guests to assemble the ingredients in the tortillas like a taco.

Serves 4

- 2 cups Cochinita Pibil (page 28)
- 8 large eggs
- 8 (6-inch) corn or flour tortillas
- ¼ cup Pickled Red Onions (page 24)
- 4 teaspoons finely chopped fresh cilantro
- 1 cup Guacamole (page 40)

Preheat the oven to 400°F.

Place ½ cup of Cochinita Pibil in the bottom of 4 oven-proof ramekins or mini cast-iron skillets. Use your fingers to spread out the Cochinita Pibil to form a large hole in the middle. Carefully crack two eggs into each hole. Transfer to the oven and bake until the whites of the eggs are set, about 14 minutes.

While the eggs are cooking, heat the tortillas in a skillet over medium heat until warm and pliable. Remove from heat and place inside a tortilla warmer or inside a cloth to retain the heat.

Remove the ramekins from the oven, place the Pickled Red Onions on top of the eggs, and garnish with the cilantro. Serve with the tortillas and a side of Guacamole.

The Flavors of the Yucatán

I find the Yucatán Peninsula to be one of the most inspiring places I've experienced. The land itself is unlike anywhere else—rugged yet fertile, shaped by ancient limestone and rich with cenotes and the spirit of the people. The flavors that come from this land are bold, deep, and rooted in Mayan tradition. Ingredients like achiote, sour oranges, and habaneros aren't just flavors—they're expressions of the region's vibrant culture and history.

What makes Yucatán cuisine truly special is how it draws from the environment. Underground cooking methods like pib (earth ovens) give dishes like cochinita pibil their smoky, tender depth. The tropical heat and humidity push preservation techniques like pickling and curing to the forefront, enhancing everything from onions to fish.

When I cook with ingredients from the Yucatán—whether it's recado negro, fresh epazote, or even chaya leaves—I'm not just creating a meal. I'm telling a story of resilience, tradition, and the incredible bond between land and flavor.

Chaya Leaves

Frituras Mixtas Jaguar

RUSTIC JAGUAR HASH

Our yuca, chorizo, and plantain hash is a vibrant fusion of bold flavors and hearty textures that is absolutely delicious. The crisp edges of fried yuca and sweet plantains contrast beautifully with the savory, spiced chorizo. Each bite is rich and satisfying, balancing sweetness and spice. We like to serve this breakfast dish with a side of our tangy Mojo Guava Sauce, creating a tropical indulgence—bright, fruity, and slightly acidic, it cuts through the richness perfectly. The next time you're looking for a comforting, flavor-packed dish that brings warmth and joy with every bite, try our Jaguar Hash.

Serves 4

MOJO GUAVA SAUCE
Makes about 4 cups

1 cup guava pulp

½ cup orange juice

½ cup white vinegar

2 cups brisket braising liquid (page 42)

JAGUAR HASH

2 quarts canola oil, for frying

1 cup yuca, cut into 1-inch sticks

1 cup chorizo, cut into 1-inch pieces

1 cup plantain, cut into 1-inch pieces

Kosher salt, for seasoning

4 large eggs, optional

2 tablespoons chopped fresh Italian flat-leaf parsley

2 cups Mojo Guava Sauce

To make the Mojo Guava Sauce: Add the guava pulp, orange juice, vinegar, and reserved brisket braising liquid to a saucepan or stockpot. Warm gently over medium heat, stirring until blended and heated through, then serve.

Add the canola oil to a deep-sided frying pan or pot set over medium-high heat. Bring the oil temperature up to 350°F. Use a candy thermometer to check the temperature. When the oil is ready, add the yuca, chorizo, and plantain and fry, turning occasionally, until golden brown, about 4 minutes. Use a kitchen spider or mesh skimmer to remove. Drain on paper towels, then divide among 4 serving bowls. Season with salt. Top each bowl with a fried egg, if desired. Garnish with parsley and serve with Mojo Guava Sauce on the side.

Fruta Fresca con Nueces Caramelizadas, Coco, y Queso Cottage

FRESH FRUIT WITH CARAMELIZED NUTS, COCONUT & COTTAGE CHEESE

What better way to brighten a morning than with a fresh fruit platter bursting with vibrant colors and tropical flavors? Depending on the season and availability, our fruit platters vary, from juicy mangoes, pineapples, papayas, and bananas, to berries, melons, and exotic fruits like dragon or passion. Regardless of the fruit we showcase, each bite offers a sweet, sun-kissed taste. The addition of caramelized nuts brings a delightful crunch and rich, sugary depth to the plate, while the toasted coconut adds warmth and texture, evoking beachside bliss. We also like to add creamy cottage cheese to our platters to balance the sweetness with a savory, tangy contrast. Altogether, our fruit platters are a refreshing, satisfying fusion of textures and flavors that celebrate nature's bounty and Latin culinary flair.

Serves 4

CARAMELIZED NUTS
Makes 4 cups

2 cups sliced almonds

1 cup hazelnuts

1 cup pumpkin seeds

½ cup sugar

¼ cup Cointreau (or triple sec)

FRUIT PLATTER

1 cup coconut flakes

3 to 4 slices fresh pineapple

3 to 4 slices fresh cantaloupe and/or honeydew

3 to 4 slices fresh watermelon

1 dragon fruit, peeled and cubed ½-inch thick

2 kiwi fruit, peeled and sliced

1 cup cottage cheese

8 hulled strawberries (halved if large)

8 blackberries

Begin by making the Caramelized Nuts: Preheat the oven to 300°F. Once the oven is pre-heated, add the almonds, hazelnuts, and pumpkin seeds, sugar, and Cointreau to a large bowl. Mix until combined. Spread out the mixture onto a lined (or greased) baking sheet and toast in the oven until golden and firm, about 15 minutes. Let cool and break into desired pieces or clusters as needed. Set aside. (Note: This recipe makes 4 cups, but the recipe

(Continued . . .)

only calls for 1–2 cups, so you can either halve the recipe or you can save some for a snack!)

Next, prepare and assemble your fruit platter: Preheat the oven to 325°F. Cover a baking sheet with parchment paper and spread the coconut flakes evenly over the paper. Toast in the oven until golden brown, about 5 minutes. **Note:** You can open the oven every two minutes to check and mix the coconut with a large spoon or tongs if the flakes are browning unevenly. Remove and let cool to room temperature.

Arrange the pineapple, cantaloupe, and watermelon slices in a triangle pattern on each of 4 individual serving plates. Divide the dragon fruit among the plates and place on top of the sliced fruit. Divide the kiwi fruit slices among the plates and place on top of the dragon fruit or on the side. Top each plate of fruit with an equal amount of cottage cheese, garnish the plates with the strawberries, blackberries, 1–2 cups Caramelized Nuts, and toasted coconut flakes, and serve.

The Fruits of Latin America

I find the fruits of Latin America to be some of the most vibrant and inspiring ingredients in the world. Each region offers a colorful palette of flavors, textures, and aromas that bring dishes to life in ways few other ingredients can. From the sweet, floral notes of guava and passion fruit to the tart punch of lulo or tamarind, Latin American fruit tells a story of biodiversity and tradition.

I'm constantly amazed by the versatility of fruits like mango, papaya, and pineapple—used in everything from breakfast dishes and savory ceviches to decadent desserts. Then there are the lesser-known gems like cherimoya, mamey, and camu camu, each with its own unique culinary potential. These fruits not only add flavor but also connect us to the land and the communities that cultivate them.

Working with fresh Latin American fruit allows me to explore a deeper connection to heritage, seasonality, and creativity in the kitchen. Whether blended into juices, incorporated into salsas, or served fresh on our platters to showcase their natural brilliance, these fruits elevate cuisine beyond nourishment—they create an experience. As a chef, I see them as essential tools in telling a cultural story through food.

Huevos Rancheros

RANCH-STYLE EGGS

As you may be familiar, Huevos Rancheros is a traditional Mexican breakfast showcasing fried eggs served on lightly fried corn tortillas, topped with a flavorful tomato-chili sauce. Our hearty and delicious version—a popular breakfast and brunch special of ours—features our homemade Salsa Ranchera, Black Beans, and fresh cilantro. The vibrant dish reflects its rural origins, providing a robust and satisfying meal that has gained popularity beyond Mexico.

Serves 4

¼ cup Merken Oil (page 22), divided

8 (6-inch) corn tortillas

8 large eggs

2 cups Salsa Ranchera (page 72), heated

¾ cup Black Beans (page 48), heated

¼ cup finely chopped fresh cilantro

¾ cup crumbled cotija cheese

Add 2 tablespoons of Merken Oil to a large skillet over medium-high heat. When the oil is heated, add the tortillas and cook for 1 minute. Flip and cook the other side until the tortilla is hot, but not hard. The edges should be lighly crispy. Remove the tortillas and set aside. Add the remaining 2 tablespoons of Merken Oil to the skillet. When the oil is heated, add the eggs and fry sunny side up. Remove from the heat and set aside.

Place two tortillas on each serving plate, with one tortilla on top of the other. Add 2 fried eggs to the top of each tortilla stack. Top each stack with ½ cup of the Salsa Ranchera while avoiding covering the yolks. Place about 3 tablespoons of Black Beans on the side of each plate. Garnish with cilantro, sprinkle the cheese over the eggs, and serve.

Pan con Maduros

CUSTARD BREAD WITH SWEET PLANTAINS & DULCE DE LECHE WHIPPED CREAM

Like French toast, this delightful Central American breakfast specialty features thick brioche that's crunchy like a churro and moist and creamy from the custard made from dulce de leche flavored with plantains. At Jaguar, we enjoy working with plantains because they offer a very Latin-tropical flavor. The brioche, the star ingredient in this dish, should not be too spongy. If it is, simply dry it in a 350°F oven for 10 minutes.

Serves 4

CUSTARD BREAD WITH SWEET PLANTAINS
Makes 2 cups

1 cup whole milk

¼ cup condensed milk

¼ teaspoon pure vanilla extract

¼ teaspoon ground cinnamon

½ cup sliced ripe plantains

4 eggs

¼ teaspoon kosher salt

4 thick slices brioche, cut in half

FLOUR MIX
Makes 2 cups

½ cup all-purpose flour

½ cup cornstarch

½ teaspoon granulated sugar

½ teaspoon ground cinnamon

1 cup panko breadcrumbs

DULCE DE LECHE WHIPPED CREAM
Makes 2 cups

½ cup heavy cream

⅛ teaspoon kosher salt

1 cup mascarpone

½ cup dulce de leche

¼ teaspoon ground cinnamon

OTHER

2 cups vegetable oil

4 cups sliced sweet ripe plantain

½ cup powdered sugar

To make the Custard Bread with Sweet Plantains: Add the milk, condensed milk, vanilla, cinnamon, plantains, eggs, and salt to a blender. Blend until smooth. Transfer the mixture to a high-sided baking sheet pan and add the slices of brioche. Allow the brioche to soak up the mixture, then turn the slices over so the other side absorbs the mixture, about 10 minutes total. Make sure not to allow the slices to sit in the mixture for too long, otherwise they may not hold together. Keep refrigerated until ready to use.

To make the Flour Mix: Add the flour, cornstarch, sugar, cinnamon, and breadcrumbs to a large bowl. Mix well to combine and set aside until ready to use.

To make the Dulce de Leche Whipped Cream: Add the heavy cream and salt to a large bowl and whip until the cream doubles in volume. Fold in the marscapone and mix softly with a rubber spatula until incorporated. Fold in the dulce de leche and mix softly until incorporated, then mix in the cinnamon. Refrigerate until ready to use.

To finish the dish: Add the 2 cups vegetable oil to a large deep-sided pan over medium-high heat and heat until the temperature registers 375°F. Use a candy thermometer to check the temperature.

While the oil is heating, add the cut slices of the brioche to the bowl with the Flour Mix and coat well. Then carefully place the slices in the hot oil (cook in batches to not overcrowd the pan). Fry for 2½ to 3 minutes, or until golden brown. Using a pair of tongs, carefully turn over the slices and fry the other side for another 2½ to 3 minutes, or until golden brown and crispy. Remove from the oil and place on a paper towel–lined plate to drain. Repeat with the remaining slices.

Divide the fried Custard Bread among 4 individual plates. Top with the sliced sweet ripe plantain and Whipped Cream. Garnish with the powdered sugar and serve.

STREET FARE

We enjoy bringing the heartbeat of Latin America's bustling streets into the Jaguar kitchen with a menu inspired by the region's vibrant street food culture. Every dish reflects the bold flavors, lively spirit, and culinary creativity found from Mexico City to Buenos Aires. With Bolivia's sweet and savory chicken empanadas, Nicaragua's crispy Vigorón (Pork Belly), and Peru's sizzling Anticuchos (Grilled Beef Skewers), we believe we do a fine job of capturing the soul of street food—fresh, fast, and full of character. Each bite tells a story of local ingredients, time-honored traditions, and the diverse communities that define Latin American cuisine. Whether it's fresh Tacos de Pescado (Fish Tacos) from Mexico or the classic Cuban Ham Sandwich from Cuba, the tempting bites you'll find throughout this chapter celebrate the essence of eating on the go, where flavor is king and every meal is a shared experience. Our creations invite you to explore the streets of Latin America, one delicious bite at a time—no passport required.

Anticuchos Peruanos de Res

PERUVIAN GRILLED BEEF SKEWERS

Anticuchos are a popular Peruvian street food, consisting of marinated meat skewers, traditionally made with beef heart. Originating from the time of the Spanish conquest, this dish blends Indigenous ingredients with African culinary influences. The meat is marinated in a mixture of vinegar, garlic, cumin, and aji panca, a smoky red chili pepper, before being grilled over an open flame. Anticuchos are often served with potatoes and a spicy dipping sauce, which is how we prepare it at Jaguar. Enjoy these mouthwatering skewers, which are a beloved part of Peruvian cuisine, known for their bold flavors and strong ties to the country's cultural heritage.

Serves 4

MARINADE

¼ cup aji panca paste

3 garlic cloves, peeled and chopped

2 tablespoons olive oil

½ cup apple cider vinegar

1 teaspoon ground cumin

1 teaspoon ground oregano

1 teaspoon kosher salt

BEEF SKEWERS

1 pound beef tenderloin, cut into 1½ inch cubes

2 cups creamer (or baby gold) potatoes, cooked and cut in half

1 cup Aji Panca Sauce (page 32)

1 cup Salsa Criolla Roja (page 32)

To make the Marinade: Add the aji panca paste, garlic, olive oil, vinegar, cumin, oregano, and salt to a bowl. Mix until incorporated. Add the beef cubes and potatoes and refrigerate for 1 to 3 hours.

Preheat an outdoor grill to medium-high heat.

Using 8 pre-soaked bamboo skewers, skewer the beef and potatoes, alternating between the two. Season with salt and brush with the remaining marinade in the bowl.

Place the skewers on the grill and cook, turning the skewers throughout the grilling process, until the meat and potatoes are nicely charred on all sides and the meat is cooked to medium-rare or your desired doneness.

Transfer the skewers to a large platter. Pour the Aji Panca Sauce into a small bowl and place in the center for dipping. Garnish the skewers with a drizzle of Salsa Criolla Roja and serve.

A Closer Look at Latin American Street Fare

Latin American street fare has deep roots in the region's history, blending Indigenous, European, African, and Asian influences into vibrant, flavorful dishes that tell stories of migration, survival, and celebration. If you ask me, I find street food to be the purest expression of a culture's palate—accessible, dynamic, and rooted in tradition. From the bustling arepa stands of Venezuela and Colombia to the taco carts of Mexico and empanada vendors across Argentina and Chile, every bite is a reflection of centuries of culinary evolution.

Street fare gained popularity due to its affordability and convenience, especially in urban centers where workers and students needed fast, satisfying meals. Over time, these humble offerings became beloved national icons. Dishes like elotes (grilled corn slathered with cheese and chili) and anticuchos (grilled beef skewers) showcase the creativity of cooks who transform simple ingredients into unforgettable experiences.

Today, Latin American street food enjoys international acclaim, embraced by food lovers and chefs worldwide for its bold flavors and cultural depth. Pop-ups, food trucks, and upscale restaurants often reinterpret these classics, but their soul remains the same: food made with heart, meant to be shared. Whether I'm preparing pupusas, ceviche, or tamales at Jaguar, I'm constantly reminded this cuisine is not only delicious but deeply communal. It brings people together, transcending borders and language, and that's what makes it so powerful—and so popular. As a chef, I can find no greater inspiration than that.

Arepas
HANDMADE CORN CAKES

Arepas are a traditional dish from Venezuela and Colombia, made from ground maize or maize flour. These round, flat cakes are grilled, baked, or fried and have a slightly crispy exterior with a soft, doughy interior. Arepas can be eaten plain or stuffed with a variety of fillings, such as cheese or meat. I like Braised Brisket (page 42) or chicken, Black Beans (page 48), and avocado or freshly made Guacamole (page 40). Arepas are incredibly versatile, enjoyed at any meal, and customized to personal tastes. Arepas have ancient origins, dating back to pre-Columbian times, and are cherished today for their simplicity, adaptability, and cultural significance in both Venezuela and Colombia.

Serves 4

- 1 cup masa harina corn flour
- 1 cup water
- 2 tablespoons softened unsalted butter
- 1 teaspoon kosher salt

Preheat the oven to 350°F.

Add the masa harina, water, butter, and salt to a medium bowl. Knead the mixture for about 5 minutes until a soft dough forms. Let the dough rest for 5 minutes. **Note:** If you find the dough a bit dry, add a little more water until you get a soft uniform dough, but make sure the dough isn't too tacky and doesn't stick to your fingers.

Divide the dough into 4 even-sized balls, a little larger than a golf ball. Flatten each dough ball with your hands and roll or press the dough until each is a ½-inch thick disk. Set aside.

Heat a large cast-iron skillet or pan over medium-high heat. When heated, add the dough disks and fry for 3 minutes on each side. **Note:** You may have to fry in batches, depending on the size of your pan.

Transfer the disks to a greased sheet pan and bake for 7 minutes, or until puffed and the crust is golden brown. Let cool.

Fill with your desired ingredients and serve.

Arepa Abierta Reina Pepiada

OPEN-FACED CURVY QUEEN AREPA

Like the Arepa recipe on the previous page, these open-faced arepas—named in honor of Susana Duijm, the first Venezuelan woman to be crowned Miss World—are equally delightful and pair perfectly with savory or sweet fillings. Whether stuffed with cheese, shredded meats, avocado, or eggs, arepas can be easily customized to suit individual tastes. In this recipe, we top our open-faced arepa with avocado, shredded chicken, and Repollo (Pickled Slaw), page 128. Simple yet rich, open-faced arepas are pure culinary joy.

Serves 4

- 4 avocados, chopped
- 2 cups cooked and shredded chicken breast
- ½ cup mayonnaise
- ¼ cup heavy cream
- ½ cup finely chopped white onion
- 1 teaspoon minced garlic
- ½ cup chopped fresh cilantro
- ¼ cup lime juice
- Kosher salt, to taste
- Unsalted butter or canola oil, for frying
- 4 arepas
- 1 cup Repollo (Pickled Slaw, page 128)

Add the avocados, chicken, mayonnaise, cream, onion, garlic, cilantro, and lime juice to a large mixing bowl. Mix well and season with salt to taste. Refrigerate until ready to serve.

Add a little butter or canola oil to a large cast-iron skillet or pan over medium-high heat. When heated, add the arepas and fry on both sides until hot and crunchy, about 5 minutes per side. Remove and place 1 arepa on each individual serving plate. Top each arepa with an equal amount of the chilled chicken mixture, garnish with the Repollo, and serve.

Choripán

ARGENTINE CHORIZO SANDWICH

Choripán, which I like to call the cousin of the American hot dog, is a beloved street food originating from Argentina, and popular across Latin America. The name comes from its two main ingredients: "chorizo" (a flavorful, spiced sausage) and "pan" (bread). The chorizo is grilled until slightly crispy and then served inside a crusty bread, like a baguette. Chimichurri, a tangy and herbaceous sauce made with parsley, garlic, vinegar, and olive oil, gives the chorizo extra flavor. Choripán is typically eaten as a quick snack or appetizer at barbecues (asados) and is a favorite during sporting events and festivals for its simplicity and satisfying taste.

Serves 4

CHIMICHURRI

1 cup chopped fresh Italian flat-leaf parsley

¼ cup dried oregano (soaked in ½ cup boiled water for 10 minutes)

1 teaspoon red chili pepper flakes

1 teaspoon smoked paprika

5 garlic cloves, peeled and minced

½ cup red wine vinegar

1 cup grapeseed oil

Kosher salt and fresh cracked black pepper, to taste

ARGENTINE CHORIZO SANDWICH

4 Argentine chorizo links

4 mini baguettes

To make the Chimichurri: Add the parsley, oregano with hot water, chili flakes, paprika, garlic, vinegar, and oil to a bowl. Whisk until incorporated. Season with salt and pepper and set aside.

Preheat an outdoor grill to medium heat.

Place the chorizo links on the heated grill. **Note:** If desired, you can also split the chorizo links lengthwise, being careful not to slice all the way through, and place them split side down on the grill. Turn the links occasionally, until slightly charred on both sides and cooked through, 20 to 25 minutes. Set the chorizo links away from the heat while toasting the baguettes. Split the baguettes and toast on the grill.

To assemble, arrange the toasted baguettes on a platter or individual serving plates. Add a grilled chorizo link to each baguette, spoon the Chimichurri over the top, and serve.

More About Chorizo

I've always been drawn to Argentina's iconic chorizo. Though chorizo has its roots in Spain, Argentina has made this sausage uniquely its own. Brought over by Spanish colonizers in the 16th century, chorizo evolved in Argentina to suit local tastes and ingredients. Unlike the dry, cured Spanish versions, Argentine chorizo is typically fresh and made from a blend of ground pork, garlic, paprika, wine, and regional spices. The result is a rich, savory sausage with a bold, smoky flavor that's both rustic and deeply satisfying.

In Argentina, chorizo is far more than just a food—it's a cultural staple. You'll find it sizzling on grills at family barbecues, or as the star in our beloved choripán, that simple sandwich with chorizo on crusty bread, topped with chimichurri. Whether eaten at street corners or high-end restaurants, choripán has become a national obsession.

The popularity of Argentine chorizo continues to grow beyond its borders, gaining fans worldwide for its depth of flavor and versatility. For me, cooking with chorizo is about honoring a long-standing tradition, connecting with community, and celebrating the rich culinary heritage of Argentina.

Salteñas

BOLIVIAN CHICKEN EMPANADAS

Bolivian chicken empanadas, known as "salteñas," are a popular street food, enjoyed for their unique sweet and savory flavor combination. These baked pastries have a golden, slightly sweet dough, filled with a juicy, flavorful stew-like mixture of shredded chicken, potatoes, peas, and hard-boiled eggs. The filling is often seasoned with cumin, aji peppers, and other spices, giving it a rich, complex taste. Salteñas are notable for their filling, often containing a broth or gravy that bursts with flavor. They are typically enjoyed as a snack or light meal, especially in the mornings, and are a beloved part of Bolivian cuisine.

Serves 4

1 tablespoon olive oil

4 chicken thighs, chopped

Kosher salt, to taste

1 yellow or white onion, peeled and diced

3 garlic cloves, peeled and minced

1½ cups chicken stock

1 tablespoon unflavored gelatin (if using store-bought stock)

1 tablespoon aji panca paste

½ teaspoon ground cumin

¼ teaspoon fresh cracked black pepper

½ russet potato, peeled and chopped small

¼ cup raisins

½ cup frozen peas

¼ cup diced kalamata olives

1 cup sliced green onions, both green and white parts

2 hardboiled eggs, sliced

4 to 6 premade empanada pastry doughs

Add the oil to a Dutch oven or large saucepan over medium-high heat. When the oil is hot and shimmering, add the chicken, season with salt, and cook, turning occasionally, for 2 minutes. Add the onions and garlic and continue cooking, stirring occasionally, until the onions are translucent and have slightly caramelized, about 5 minutes. Add the chicken stock and stir to incorporate. **Note:** If you're using homemade chicken stock, you can omit the gelatin. Otherwise, add the gelatin to the store-bought stock and mix well before adding to the pan. Add the aji panca, cumin, pepper, potato, and raisins, and cook until the potato is cooked through, about 7 minutes. Check the seasoning, adjust if necessary, and turn off the heat. Stir in the peas, olives, and green onions.

Transfer the mixture into a large greased shallow casserole dish. Let cool to room temperature.

Preheat the oven to 350°F.

Place 4 to 6 of the premade empanada pastry doughs on a clean smooth surface. Spoon the cooled filling mixture on one side of the flat doughs. Add a slice or two of hard-boiled egg, then fold the empanada. Lift the empanada and make it stand with the flat side down and the round part up. Use your fingers to pinch the empanada tightly closed along the edges. Transfer to a greased baking sheet.

Bake until hot and golden brown, about 15 to 20 minutes. Remove and let cool slightly before serving.

More About the Empanada

Like most of the classic and traditional dishes throughout this book, I find Bolivia's empanadas to be a perfect blend of tradition, flavor, and cultural identity. They trace their roots to colonial times, when Spanish settlers introduced filled pastries. Over generations, Indigenous ingredients and cooking techniques transformed the empanada into something uniquely Bolivian. Today's empanada is a slightly sweet, golden pastry filled with a juicy stew of beef or chicken, potatoes, peas, and a hint of spice, often thickened with gelatin so the broth doesn't spill while eating.

Empanadas are incredibly popular across Bolivia, enjoyed as a mid-morning snack or light meal. Each region adds its own twist—some include olives, boiled eggs, or raisins—showcasing the country's diverse palate. Street vendors and bakeries sell them fresh daily, and they're a staple at family gatherings and celebrations. Their popularity lies not only in their rich flavor but also in their practicality—portable, affordable, and deeply satisfying. As a chef, I admire how empanadas in Bolivia reflect both history and innovation, passed down through generations and still evolving today. They represent the heart of Bolivian cuisine: humble ingredients elevated through time, care, and culture.

Sandwich Cubano

CUBAN HAM SANDWICH

The Cuban sandwich, or "Cubano," is a popular sandwich that originated in Florida's Cuban communities. It typically consists of Cuban bread filled with roast pork, ham, Swiss cheese, pickles, and mustard. Our version of the Cubano includes our tender Pork Shoulder and homemade Pickled Slaw instead of the traditional pickles for a satisfying, flavorful bite. We then press the sandwich until the bread is crisp and the cheese is melted. The Cuban sandwich has become a beloved part of Florida's food culture, symbolizing its rich immigrant history and one you'll enjoy time and time again either at Jaguar or in your own kitchen.

Serves 4

- 1 loaf (6 to 8 slices) Cuban bread
- 4 tablespoons yellow mustard
- 6 slices Swiss cheese
- 6 slices deli honey ham
- 6 slices Pork Shoulder (page 220)
- ¾ cup Repollo (Pickled Slaw, page 128)
- 2 tablespoons softened unsalted butter

Preheat a panini press or large cast-iron skillet or pan to medium heat. **Note:** If using a skillet or pan, have a bacon press ready to press the sandwich.

For each sandwich, layer the bottom slice of the bread with mustard, then add the cheese. Top the cheese with the ham, followed by the sliced pork and the Pickled Slaw. Top with a slice of bread. Rub the top and bottom side of the bread with the softened butter and place in either the panini press or the skillet or pan. Use the bacon press to press the sandwich while it cooks if not using the panini press. You'll also have to cook each side for 3 minutes, or until the bread is golden brown and crunchy and the cheese has melted. Remove, slice in half, and serve.

Brief History of the Cuban Sandwich

Because I have a genuine interest in culinary history, I find the story of the Cuban sandwich—also known as the Cubano—as rich as its flavors. Originating from Cuban communities in Florida in the late 1800s to early 1900s, the sandwich was a staple for Cuban workers in cigar factories in Key West and later in Tampa and Miami. Though its exact birthplace is still debated, its roots are unmistakably tied to the Cuban immigrant experience.

The traditional Cuban sandwich is built on Cuban bread, crisp on the outside and airy inside. It's layered with mojo-marinated roast pork, sweet ham, Swiss cheese, pickles, and yellow mustard. In Tampa, salami is also included—an influence from the city's large Italian population—adding a unique twist. The sandwich is then pressed on a plancha, melding all the ingredients into a warm, flavorful harmony.

For me, the Cuban sandwich tells a story of cultural fusion and adaptation. It reflects how immigrants shaped local cuisine while preserving their heritage. Today, it's more than just a meal—it's a symbol of resilience, community, and flavor. Whether you're in a corner café in Little Havana or at a food truck in Tampa, the Cubano is a timeless classic worth celebrating.

Tacos de Pescado con Repollo

FISH TACOS WITH COLESLAW

Our fish tacos, featuring fresh mahi mahi and homemade coleslaw, are a mouthwatering delight. The tender, flaky fish is perfectly seasoned and grilled to bring out its mild, slightly sweet flavor. Paired with crisp, tangy coleslaw, each bite offers a satisfying contrast of textures and tastes. The freshness of the cabbage and creamy dressing further balance the richness of the fish, while warm tortillas hold it all together. These tacos are a fresh, flavorful explosion perfect for any meal.

Serves 4 (2 tacos per serving)

- 1 pound fresh boneless, skinless mahi mahi fillet, butterflied or thinly sliced
- ½ cup Merken Confit (page 22)
- 2 tablespoons chopped fresh Italian flat-leaf parsley, divided
- Kosher salt, to taste
- 2 cups Coleslaw (page 58)
- 1 cup Aji Amarillo Aioli (page 32)
- 3 tablespoons vegetable oil
- 8 (6-inch) flour tortillas
- 2 limes, cut in half
- 1 cup Chipotle Aioli (page 42)

Add the mahi mahi to a large bowl along with the Merken Confit and half the parsley, and season with salt. Mix until the mahi mahi is well covered, and set aside to marinate.

Add the Coleslaw to a medium bowl, add the remaining parsley, and season with salt. Mix until incorporated, then add the Aji Amarillo Aioli and mix again. Set aside.

Add about 3 tablespoons oil to a large cast-iron skillet or pan over medium-high heat. When the oil is hot and shimmering, add the fish and sear for about 1½ minutes, give or take, depending on the thickness of the fillet. With a fish spatula, turn the fish over and cook for about 1 minute. Be careful not to overcook. Remove and let the fish rest. Wipe the skillet or pan clean, place back over the heat, and add the tortillas (in batches) to warm. Remove the tortillas.

Add 2 tortillas to each serving plate. Top with equal amounts of the dressed Coleslaw. Cut the fish into 8 even pieces and place each piece on top of the Coleslaw. Garnish the plates with a half of lime and serve immediately with a side of Chipotle Aioli.

Why Mahi Mahi?

If you've been to Jaguar and perused our menu, you know we love featuring mahi mahi. That's because the fish has a firm, lean texture that holds up beautifully to almost any of our preparations—grilling, pan-searing, and baking. Mahi's mild, slightly sweet flavor makes it incredibly versatile and appealing to a wide range of palates, even for our guests who don't usually order seafood.

Personally, I find mahi to be one of those ingredients that lets me get creative. It pairs wonderfully with tropical fruits like mango or pineapple, citrus-based sauces, and bold seasonings like chili or jerk spice. It also plays well with Mediterranean or Asian-inspired flavors, making it a favorite when I want to experiment.

Beyond its taste and texture, mahi cooks quickly and evenly, making it ideal for busy kitchens or home cooks wanting to impress without stress. It looks beautiful on the plate, too—with its flaky, white flesh and golden sear, it's visually appealing.

And let's not forget—mahi is a more sustainable choice compared to many other popular fish. When sourced responsibly, it's a great way to enjoy seafood with a clearer conscience. For all these reasons, mahi is a staple I never get tired of working with.

Vigorón con Repollo

YUCA, PORK BELLY & PORK RINDS WITH PICKLED SLAW

Vigorón is a traditional Nicaraguan dish known for its simplicity and bold flavors. Typically served on a banana leaf, it consists of boiled yuca (cassava) topped with chicharrón (crispy fried pork rinds) and a tangy cabbage slaw referred to as Repollo or Curtido. The slaw is made from cabbage, tomatoes, and onions lightly dressed with vinegar for a refreshing contrast to the hearty pork and starchy yuca. Vigorón is often enjoyed as a street food or casual meal, especially in cities like Granada. Its combination of textures and flavors makes it a beloved comfort food in Nicaraguan cuisine.

Serves 4

YUCA, PORK BELLY, AND PORK RINDS

1 pound yuca, cleaned and chopped into bite-sized pieces

1 cup Pork Belly (page 216), chopped into bite-sized pieces

1 cup chicharrónes pork rinds, chopped into bite-sized pieces

REPOLLO (PICKLED SLAW)

1 cup shredded green or red cabbage

½ cup shredded carrot

½ cup diced tomato

¼ cup finely chopped red onion

2 tablespoons red wine vinegar

2 tablespoons olive oil

½ cup chopped fresh cilantro

½ teaspoon crushed coriander seeds

1 habanero pepper, cut in half

Kosher salt and fresh cracked black pepper, to taste

Bring a stockpot of salted water to a boil over high heat. Once boiling, add the chopped yuca. Boil until the yuca is soft, about 15 minutes. Drain the yuca and set aside.

Heat a large cast-iron skillet to medium-high heat. When heated, add the chopped Pork Belly and pork rinds. Sear, stirring occasionally, until the pork and rinds are crispy and golden brown, about 20 minutes. Remove the pork and rinds and set aside.

To make the Pickled Slaw: Add the cabbage, carrot, tomato, onion, vinegar, oil, cilantro, coriander, and habanero to a mixing bowl. Toss well until combined. Season to taste with salt and pepper.

To assemble, spoon the yuca, pork belly, and pork rinds on individual serving plates. Top with the pickled slaw and serve.

TRADITIONAL & INFLUENTIAL PLATES

Welcome to a journey through the rich, diverse flavors of Latin America—an ever-evolving cuisine rooted in tradition, shaped by geography, and alive with cultural expression. In the chapters ahead, I'll guide you through dishes inspired by the land and sea, by ancient customs and modern influences, all brought together by a love for bold ingredients and honest cooking.

From the lush forests and vibrant gardens come recipes that honor the earth: hearty root vegetables, fragrant herbs, tropical fruits, and ancestral grains. You'll find inspiration in dishes that are simple yet deeply nourishing, celebrating the gifts of the land.

Next, we travel to the oceans and coastlines, where the flavors turn fresh and briny—think ceviches kissed with citrus, fresh grilled mahi mahi, and tender shrimp with garlic and guajillo chiles. These coastal recipes reflect the rhythm of the tides and the bounty they bring.

From the farms and pastures, we embrace the heartier side of Latin American cooking—slow-cooked meats, succulent pork dishes, and comforting chicken combinations, all steeped in time-honored techniques passed down through generations.

And of course, no journey is complete without something sweet. The final chapter brings an indulgent assortment of desserts, from a silky flan and creamy cheesecake to a festive chocolate cake and banana crepes meant to be shared.

Each recipe is a window into a place, a people, and a memory. Let these chapters be your guide to cooking with soul, pride, and deep cultural respect.

Forest & Garden

At Jaguar, we enjoy drawing inspiration from the lush forests and vibrant gardens of Latin America to create dishes that are as nourishing as they are flavorful. Using ingredients sourced from nature's bounty—from wild herbs and native fruits to heirloom vegetables and edible flowers—we craft meals that honor the land's richness and cultural roots. Our cuisine also celebrates the deep connection between food and the earth, weaving together ancestral knowledge with modern creativity. Imagine dishes infused with the citrusy tang of Amazonian camu camu, the earthy depth of root vegetables like yuca, and the fragrant touch of fresh cilantro and sunflower shoots. Each plate featured in this exciting chapter reflects the rhythms of the natural world, with flavors that are wild, pure, and deeply satisfying. With every bite, we invite you to explore the forests and gardens of Latin America—places where the inhabitants strive to honor tradition, use resources wisely, and bring flavors together in perfect harmony.

Arroz Chaufa

CHINESE PERUVIAN FRIED RICE

Arroz Chaufa—a dish our guests are very familiar with—is a flavorful fusion of Chinese and Peruvian cuisine, bursting with savory goodness. I find it to be the perfect balance of tender rice, juicy Choclo, and stir-fried vegetables, all seasoned with our Lomo Sauce. The smoky aroma and rich flavors make it irresistibly satisfying. Its slightly crispy texture from the wok adds depth, while the mix of ingredients creates a comforting, hearty dish. At Jaguar, we'll serve this dish topped with a fried egg and drizzle of Aji Panca Sauce.

Serves 4

SWEET POTATO
Makes 4 cups

4 cups sweet potato, peeled and cut in 1-inch cubes

1 cup orange juice

1 cup water

4 tablespoons brown sugar

1 star anise

1 tablespoon salt

HOUSE WHITE RICE
Makes 8 cups

½ white onion, peeled and roughly chopped

2 cloves garlic, peeled and crushed

½ cup vegetable oil

2 tablespoons kosher salt

½ cup peeled and cubed carrots

¼ cup peas

½ cup corn kernels

½ cup russet potato wedges

2 cups uncooked jasmine rice

LOMO SAUCE
Makes about 2 cups

½ cup red wine vinegar

⅛ teaspoon ground cumin

2 teaspoons aji amarillo paste

1½ cups soy sauce

2 cloves garlic, peeled and grated

TO FINISH

4 eggs

½ cup vegetable oil

1 cup thinly sliced red onion

1 cup thinly sliced red bell pepper

1 cup cooked Choclo (page xxxiii)

1 cup small, cubed zucchini

1 cup cooked Sweet Potato

1 tablespoon kosher salt

4 cups House White Rice

½ cup Lomo Sauce

1 tablespoon sesame oil

1 cup chopped fresh cilantro

1 cup Aji Panca Sauce (page 32)

To make the Sweet Potato: Add the potatoes, orange juice, water, brown sugar, star anise, and salt to a medium-sized saucepan over high heat. Mix well and bring to a boil. Cook for 3 minutes. Turn off the heat and allow to continue to cook until soft but firm.

To make the House White Rice: Add the onion, garlic, and ½ cup water to a bowl. Mix until combined and set aside. Add the oil to a large saucepot over medium heat. When heated, add the onion-garlic mixture and cook for 5 minutes. Add 4 cups water along with the salt and bring to a boil. Add the carrots, peas, corn, potato, and rice. Reduce the heat to low, cover the pot, and cook for 25 minutes, or until the rice is tender. Remove from the heat and let the pot rest for 10 minutes. Fluff the rice with a fork just before serving.

To make the Lomo Sauce: Add the vinegar, cumin, aji amarillo paste, soy sauce, and garlic to a mixing bowl and whisk until well combined. Set aside until ready to serve.

To finish: Heat a large nonstick frying pan over medium high heat. When hot, crack the eggs and add to the pan, sunny side up. Cook to desired doneness, then remove from the heat and set aside.

Add the oil to a large wok, skillet, or pan over high heat. When oil has heated, add the onions and cook for 1 minute. Add the bell pepper, Choclo, zucchini, and Sweet Potato and cook, stirring occasionally, until slightly charred, about 3 minutes. Season with salt. Add the House White Rice and mix to incorporate. Add the Lomo Sauce and stir well. Remove from the heat and add the sesame oil and cilantro. Divide the rice among 4 serving plates and top each plate with a fried egg. Drizzle the Aji Panca Sauce around the rice and serve.

Ensalada Celia

CELIA'S SALAD

Named after Latin singer Celia Cruz, this Jaguar classic has been on our menu since the restaurant's inception. It remains one of our favorites with our guests because of the delicious combination of crisp lettuce and bell pepper, the creaminess of avocado, and the crunch of crisp tortilla strips—all tossed with a savory Black Bean Vinaigrette. For those who don't know, Celia Cruz was a legendary Cuban American singer known as the "Queen of Salsa." Her powerful voice, vibrant stage presence, and iconic catchphrase, "Azucar!" made her a global icon. She packed a punch—much like this salad.

Serves 4

CELIA DRESSING
Makes 3 cups

2 garlic cloves, peeled

½ teaspoon ground cumin

1 medium-sized jalapeño pepper

1 cup fresh cilantro leaves

1 teaspoon kosher salt

½ cup white vinegar

1½ cups vegetable oil

BLACK BEAN VINAIGRETTE
Makes 4 cups

3 cups black beans, drained, rinsed and dried with paper towel

1 cup diced fresh tomatoes

1 cup Choclo (page xxxiii)

1 cup diced red onion

1 cup fresh cilantro leaves

2 tablespoons red wine vinegar

2 tablespoons olive oil

2 tablespoons avocado oil

1 teaspoon kosher salt

CRISPY CORN TORTILLAS
Makes about 2 cups

2 medium-sized corn tortillas, cut in half and sliced into fine strips

4 cups vegetable oil

Kosher salt, as needed

CELIA'S SALAD

4 cups iceberg lettuce, thinly shredded

4 cups romaine hearts, thinly shredded

1 teaspoon kosher salt

½ cup Celia Dressing

1 red bell pepper, thinly sliced

½ cup Black Bean Vinaigrette

2 avocados, peeled and thinly sliced

Crispy Corn Tortilla strips

To make the Celia Dressing: Add the garlic, cumin, and jalapeño to a small, dry skillet or pan over medium heat. Cook, stirring occasionally, until the jalapeño and garlic have softened and have a bit of char, about 5 minutes. Remove from the heat and let cool. When cooled, remove the stem from the jalapeño, split the pepper in half, and remove the seeds and veins. Add the roasted jalapeño, garlic, and cumin to a blender along with the cilantro, salt, and vinegar. While the blender is running, add the oil in a steady stream until it's fully incorporated into the dressing. Transfer to a container and taste. Season with salt if necessary. Set aside until ready to use.

To make the Black Bean Vinaigrette: Add the beans, tomatoes, Choclo, onion, cilantro, vinegar, both oils, and salt to a large bowl. Gently toss to combine. Taste and adjust the seasoning if necessary. Transfer the dressing to a container and refrigerate until ready to use or keep in an airtight container in the refrigerator for up to 4 days.

To make the Crispy Corn Tortillas: Add the oil to a Dutch oven over medium heat. When the oil reaches 350°F (use a candy or digital thermometer to check the temperature), add the tortilla strips. Fry until golden, about 30 seconds depending on the thickness of the strips. Use a slotted spoon or spider to remove the strips. Transfer to a paper towel–lined plate to drain. Season with salt and set aside until ready to use.

To assemble Celia's Salad: Add the shredded lettuce to a large cold bowl. Season with salt. Add the Celia Dressing and bell pepper and gently toss to combine. Divide among 4 cold salad plates. Top each salad with the Black Bean Vinaigrette and avocado slices. Garnish with the Crispy Corn Tortillas and serve.

Ensalada de Carioca con Mango, Papaya, Pina, y Anacardos

CARIOCA SALAD WITH MANGO, PAPAYA, PINEAPPLE & CASHEWS

This vibrant and refreshing salad is inspired by the flavors of Brazil. It features a colorful mix of tropical fruits, like mango, papaya, and pineapple, tossed with crisp greens for a light yet satisfying base. Cashews add a rich crunch and nutty flavor, balancing the sweetness of the fruit. A citrus-lime vinaigrette ties everything together, enhancing the tropical notes. Perfect for warm weather, this salad offers a delicious blend of textures and bold, sunny flavors.

Serves 4

1 pineapple

1 tablespoon + 1 cup olive oil, divided

4 tablespoons cashews

2 tablespoons toasted coconut flakes

1 cup cubed papaya

1 cup cubed mango

2 cups mixed greens

½ cup red wine vinegar

¼ cup lime juice

Kosher salt, to taste

1 cup sunflower shoots

Peel the pineapple, then stand the flesh upright and cut in half from the top to the bottom. Cut the halves again to obtain 4 equal size wedges. Lay each wedge on its side and trim to remove the center core from each wedge. Place the trimmed wedges in the refrigerator for at least 1 hour, or until cold.

Prepare an outdoor grill to medium-high heat.

Brush a little oil (about 1 tablespoon) on each pineapple wedge and place on the grill for about 2 minutes on each side until the pineapple is nicely charred. Remove and cut into 1-inch cubes. Set aside. **Note:** Any extra pineapple can used to snack on later or placed in a blender with some ice water to make a refreshing drink.

Add the cashews to a small skillet over medium heat. Toss the nuts constantly with a wooden spoon to roast evenly, until golden and aromatic, but do not burn. Remove the cashews and set aside. Add the coconut flakes to the skillet and constantly toss with a wooden spoon to roast evenly, until golden and aromatic, but do not burn. Remove the coconut and set aside.

Add 1 cup of the grilled pineapple to a large bowl along with the papaya, mango, mixed greens, vinegar, remaining 1 cup olive oil, and lime juice. Gently mix until incorporated. Season with salt.

Divide the fruit-salad mixture among 4 individual serving plates. Garnish with the sunflower shoots, roasted cashews, and toasted coconut flakes, and serve.

Sunflower Shoots

I like using sunflower shoots because they are a vibrant, versatile ingredient that bridges tradition and innovation. While not historically prominent in Latin America, these tender greens fit seamlessly into the region's culinary ethos—fresh, bold, and rooted in the land. Their slightly nutty, peppery flavor complements staples like beans, corn, avocado, and tropical fruits. I love folding them into ceviches and salads for a crisp contrast, layering them in arepas, or using them to finish empanadas and tamales for a fresh bite. In contemporary kitchens across Latin America, chefs are embracing microgreens and shoots as part of the new wave of sustainable, farm-to-table cooking. Sunflower shoots grow quickly, require minimal resources, and pack a nutritional punch, aligning beautifully with Indigenous agricultural values. They're more than a garnish—they're a symbol of how Latin American cuisine continues to evolve while honoring its deep connection to the earth.

Sopa de Cilantro

CILANTRO SOUP

This cilantro soup of ours is another vibrant, soul-warming dish bursting with fresh, herbal flavor. The aromatic cilantro blends beautifully with onion, pepper, and spices, creating a rich broth that's comforting and invigorating. Paired with zucchini and chicken stock, and topped with crispy corn tortillas and sour cream, the soup balances earthiness with brightness. Each spoonful delivers a zesty, savory taste that lingers deliciously. It's another celebration of simple ingredients, transformed into a satisfying and culturally rich culinary experience.

Serves 4

- ½ cup unsalted butter
- ½ cup chopped white onion
- 1 teaspoon kosher salt
- 1 cup chopped zucchini
- ¼ medium-sized jalapeño pepper, de-seeding optional
- 4 cups chicken stock
- 1 cup chopped cilantro
- 1 cup Crispy Corn Tortillas (page 138)
- ¼ cup sour cream

Add the butter to a medium-sized stockpot or saucepan. When the butter has melted and is foaming, add the onion and cook until softened, about 10 minutes. Season with salt. Add the zucchini and jalapeño, and cook for 3 minutes. Add the chicken stock and cilantro, and bring to a boil. Remove from the heat and let cool. When the soup has cooled down, add to a blender and purée until smooth and creamy. **Note:** You can also use an immersion blender. Reheat the soup until hot, then divide among 4 soup bowls. Garnish with Crispy Corn Tortillas and sour cream and serve.

Sopa de Frijol Negro

BLACK BEAN SOUP

Being in Miami and surrounded by sunny skies, warm temperatures, and tropical breezes, soups aren't a huge draw, but when they are, this one and our Cilantro Soup are the two our guests will request. Our tender and creamy Black Bean Soup is rich and flavorful, and it warms the soul on any chilly day. Each spoonful offers a smoky, savory depth with a hint of heat, perfectly balanced by sour cream and fresh Pico de Gallo and cilantro. Whether served with rice or crusty bread, this comforting dish is a welcome sight when the weather turns.

Serves 4

4 cups Black Bean Purée (page 48)

1 cup Crispy Corn Tortillas (page 138)

¼ cup Pico de Gallo (page 50)

¼ cup sour cream

1 tablespoon chopped fresh cilantro

Add the Black Bean Purée to a medium-sized stockpot or saucepan placed over medium heat. When heated through, divide the purée among 4 serving bowls. Garnish with the Crispy Corn Tortillas, the Pico de Gallo on top of the tortillas, followed by the sour cream and a sprinkle of cilantro, and serve.

Soup and Latin America

I see soup as much more than a dish—it's a reflection of history, resilience, and cultural identity. Across Latin America, soup has long held a central place at the table, dating back to pre-Columbian times when Indigenous communities prepared broths from native ingredients like corn, beans, squash, and herbs. With the arrival of the Spanish and other European influences, the repertoire of soups expanded to include meats, rice, and spices, blending traditions in ways that are still evolving today.

Each region boasts its own signature soups—from Mexico's hearty pozole to Colombia's herbaceous ajiaco and Peru's chupe de camarones. These dishes are not just nourishing, they're deeply symbolic. Soup often marks celebrations, family gatherings, and even healing rituals. In many homes, it's the first thing served to welcome a guest or to bring comfort to the sick.

Soup's importance lies in its adaptability and its ability to tell a story. It uses what's local and seasonal, making it accessible to all. In the Jaguar kitchen, we treasure soup for its simplicity and complexity—it invites creativity while staying grounded in tradition. For us, soup isn't just food—it's heritage in a bowl.

Tacos de Atún en Lechuga

TUNA LETTUCE WRAPS

Tuna Lettuce Wraps—another one of our more popular dishes at Jaguar—are a refreshing and flavorful delight. Crisp lettuce cradles a savory mix of tender tuna, crisp and crunchy Coleslaw, fresh mint, and zesty Chipotle Aioli. The ensemble is a perfect demonstration of vibrant textures and balanced tastes that are light yet satisfying. The natural saltiness of the tuna pairs perfectly with the fresh, clean crunch of the lettuce. Whether as a quick lunch or a healthy snack, these wraps offer guilt-free indulgence that's as nutritious as it is delicious.

Serves 4

- 1 pound fresh tuna loin, trimmed and sliced
- 1 teaspoon kosher salt
- 4 cups Coleslaw (page 58)
- ½ tablespoon black sesame seeds
- ½ tablesooon white sesame seeds
- 4 large fresh mint leaves, chopped
- ½ cup Chipotle Aioli (page 42), plus more for serving
- 8 large Boston or butter lettuce leaves

Add the tuna to a large bowl along with the salt. Toss to combine. Add the Coleslaw, sesame seeds, mint, and Chipotle Aioli. Taste and season with salt if necessary.

Divide the lettuce leaves among 4 plates (2 leaves per plate). Divide the tuna mixture and fill the center of each leaf. Serve with extra Chipotle Aioli, if desired.

Latin American Lettuces

Boston and butter lettuces—the two lettuces we use interchangeably in our Tuna Lettuce Wraps—may not be the first ingredients that come to mind in Latin American cuisine, yet they hold unique places within regional dishes.

I often turn to Boston and butter lettuce for their unique textures and flavors. Both belong to the butterhead lettuce family and are prized for their tender, pliable leaves and mild, slightly sweet taste. In Latin American dishes, where bold flavors from citrus, chilies, and fresh herbs are common, these lettuces provide a perfect balance—cooling and crisp without overwhelming the other ingredients.

Butter lettuce is a favorite in Mexican-style tacos de lechuga, where its broad, soft leaves make ideal low-carb wrappers for fillings like spicy carne asada, shrimp a la diabla, or black bean and corn salad. Its subtle flavor allows the punch of lime and chipotle to shine through while adding a refreshing contrast.

Boston lettuce, slightly more structured yet still tender, works beautifully in layered salads and ceviche presentations across Peruvian and Central American cuisines. I use it as a base for our tuna wraps as well as citrus-marinated fish or avocado and mango combinations, where its delicate crunch elevates the dish without stealing the spotlight.

In Latin American cooking, where fresh produce and vibrant flavors are celebrated, Boston and butter lettuce are versatile staples that bring harmony and elegance to both rustic and refined plates.

Verduras Rostizadas con Garbanzos y Crema de Semillas de Calabaza

ROASTED VEGETABLES WITH CHICKPEAS AND PUMPKIN SEED SPREAD

With a vibrant fusion of flavors, this is our Latin American version of roasted vegetables. Earthy chickpeas absorb the heat and spice of the habanero while caramelized tomatoes, onions, sweet potatoes, and acorn squash bring a rich depth. Pumpkin seeds add a perfect crunch, and the fresh thyme brightens the presentation, tying together the bold and hearty elements. One bite and you'll discover the warmth, spice, and satisfying texture of this dish, which is a nourishing and flavorful tribute to Latin America.

Serves 4

PUMPKIN SEED SPREAD

2 tablespoons + ½ cup olive oil, divided

1 yellow onion, peeled and cut in quarters

1 habanero pepper, cut in half and deseeded

1 pound vine-ripened tomatoes, cut into quarters

1 cup pumpkin seeds

3 garlic cloves

Kosher salt and fresh cracked black pepper, to taste

1 cup chopped fresh cilantro

CHICKPEAS AND VEGETABLES

1 cup chickpeas

1 cup pumpkin seeds

1 cup sweet potato, peeled and cut into bite-sized cubes

1 cup beets, peeled and cut into bite-sized cubes

1 cup acorn squash, peeled and cut into bite-sized cubes

Kosher salt and fresh cracked black pepper, to taste

⅓ cup olive oil

4 thyme sprigs

2 cups Pumpkin Seed Spread

To make the Pumpkin Seed Spread: Add 2 tablespoons of olive oil to a large cast-iron skillet over medium/medium-high heat. When the oil is shimmering, add the onion, pepper, tomatoes, pumpkin seeds, and garlic. Season with salt and pepper and sauté, stirring often, until the vegetables are lightly charred around the edges, about 8 minutes. Remove from the heat and transfer the pan contents to a food processor. Pulse until a rough purée is achieved. While the machine is running, slowly drizzle in the remaining ½ cup olive oil and purée until soft. **Note:** If the mixture appears dry, add a little water to soften the mixture. Check and adjust the seasoning if necessary and transfer to a mixing bowl. Gently stir in the cilantro and set aside until ready to use.

To make the Chickpeas and Vegetables: Preheat the oven to 350°F.

Line a small sheet pan with parchment paper. Arrange the chickpeas and pumpkin seeds in an even layer. Roast until golden brown, about 5 minutes. Remove and let cool.

Line a larger sheet pan with parchment paper. Arrange the sweet potato, beets, and acorn squash in an even layer. Season with salt and pepper, and drizzle with olive oil. Add the thyme sprigs, and roast until the vegetables are brown and toasted around the edges, about 15 minutes. Carefully shake the pan or toss with a spoon to move the vegetables around. Continue to roast for another 5 minutes, or until fork tender. Remove and let cool.

Divide the Pumpkin Seed Spread among 4 serving plates, placed in the center, and spread in an artistic swoosh with the back of a spoon. Divide the roasted vegetables in the center of each plate. Garnish with the roasted chickpeas and pumpkin seeds and serve.

Oceans & Coastlines

Peek into the kitchen of Jaguar and you'll clearly see we like to dive deep into the culinary treasures of Latin America's oceans and coastlines, crafting seafood dishes that celebrate the region's rich maritime heritage. Drawing from the Pacific, Atlantic, and Caribbean shores, the creations you are about to discover in this chapter are a tribute to both tradition and the vibrant, ever-changing flavors of the sea. From our zesty ceviches of Peru to grilled mahi mahi from the Mexican coastline and Ecuadorian prawns, each dish reflects a deep respect for fresh, local ingredients and time-honored techniques. We also like to transform ocean harvests—like tender octopus, sweet shrimp, and flaky white fish—into inspired plates bursting with color and flavor. Sea salt, tropical citrus, and native chilies dance across the palate, bringing the essence of the coast to our seafood presentations. With each dish, we offer a taste of the sea's beauty and bounty, inviting you and your family and friends to experience Latin America's coasts through unforgettable cuisine.

As a chef who has spent years exploring the vibrant culinary traditions of Latin America, I've learned that few dishes capture the region's diversity and spirit quite like ceviche. This deceptively simple preparation of raw fish "cooked" in citrus juice is as rich in history as it is in flavor.

Ceviche's roots trace back over two thousand years to the coastal civilizations of present-day Peru, particularly the Moche people, who marinated fish in fermented fruit juices and local spices. With the arrival of the Spanish in the 16th century came limes and onions, transforming ceviche into a more familiar form. Peru still claims ceviche as its national dish, and its version—with fresh sea bass, lime juice, red onion, aji chili, and sweet potato—is a culinary icon.

But ceviche didn't stop at the Peruvian border. Across Latin America, the dish evolved with local ingredients and tastes. In Ecuador, it's often made with shrimp and served with popcorn or plantain chips. Mexico brings its own flair, with diced tomato, avocado, and cilantro, served atop a crisp tostada. In Chile, ceviche includes cilantro and a touch of ginger, while in Colombia, coconut milk sometimes softens the citrus tang.

What's fascinating to me as a chef is how ceviche reflects both the sea and the soul of each country. It's a dish that honors freshness, minimalism, and bold flavor—all central to Latin American cooking. And today, it's enjoying global popularity. From restaurants like Jaguar to beachside stalls, ceviche is celebrated for being light, refreshing, and healthy. The rise of fusion cuisine has also inspired new variations, blending Asian ingredients like ponzu or soy with traditional ceviche preparations.

At its core, ceviche remains a dish of the people—simple, adaptable, and deeply regional. Whether you're savoring our sweet Camaron Nuevo (Shrimp with Nuevo Sauce) or tuna-based Tiradito Lima (Delicate Raw Fish Lima-Style) ceviche, you're tasting history in every bite. For me, that's what makes ceviche not just a recipe, but a cultural treasure worth preserving and sharing.

Camaron Nuevo

SHRIMP WITH NUEVO SAUCE, MAIZ CHULPE & MERKEN OIL

This succulent shrimp ceviche features our Nuevo Sauce—one of our signature sauces at Jaguar. Our guests often recognize this dish immediately because of its vibrant yellow hue. The sauce is crafted from aji amarillo, a Peruvian yellow chili pepper. Before serving, we like to top the shrimp with Peruvian corn and a red chili oil we make in house. One bite and you'll find yourself on Barranco Beach surrounded by seaside cafés and bohemian charm.

Serves 4

NUEVO SAUCE
Makes 2 cups

1 tablespoon fresh key lime juice

2 tablespoons fresh lemon juice

1 tablespoon grated fresh ginger

2 tablespoons soy sauce

2 cloves garlic, peeled

¾ cup aji amarillo paste

1 teaspoon kosher salt

1 cup grapeseed oil

MAIZ CHULPE
Makes 4 cups

½ cup pure corn oil

4 cups Maiz Chulpe (page xxxiii)

½ cup kosher salt

OTHER

¾ pound (26/30) cooked shrimp, cut in bite-sized pieces

¼ cup Merken Oil (page 22)

To make the Nuevo Sauce: Add the lime juice, lemon juice, ginger, soy sauce, garlic, aji amarillo paste, and salt to a blender. Turn the blender on medium to blend the ingredients. When blending, slowly drizzle in the oil in a steady stream, until the sauce is thick and creamy. Remove the sauce from the blender and transfer to a glass container. Refrigerate until ready to use, for up to 1 week.

To make the Maiz Chulpe: Add the oil to a large cast-iron skillet or pan, over medium heat. Warm the oil, but do not let it smoke. Add the Maiz Chulpe while stirring constantly with a wooden spoon. **Note:** You may need to cook in batches to not overcrowd the pan. Use a frying screen so the corn doesn't fly out of the pan. Listen carefully as the dried corn starts to pop. The popping should take 5 to 6 minutes. Once all the corn has popped or imploded, season with salt and toss well. Transfer the corn to a paper towel to drain and cool before using.

To assemble: Divide the Nuevo Sauce between 4 plates and add to the center of each plate. Add the shrimp in equal amounts on top of the sauce. Sprinkle a couple tablespoons of Maiz Chulpe on top and around the shrimp. Finish with a drizzle of Merken Oil and serve.

Mercado Negro

BLACK MARKET CEVICHE

This vibrant ceviche, bursting with flavors and textures, is one of our most popular dishes. We quickly boil tender shrimp and calamari, then toss them with corvina that's been marinating in lime juice, infusing it with a refreshing tanginess. Accompanied by crisp red onion that adds a sharp bite, sweet potatoes offering a hint of sweetness, large Peruvian corn kernels for a pop of freshness, and our creamy Nuevo Sauce, each bite showcases the diversity of marine delights in a single, tantalizing dish.

Serves 4

CALAMARI AND SHRIMP

2 tablespoons kosher salt

1 bay leaf

½ lemon

½ pound raw shrimp (26/30), cleaned, peeled, and deveined

½ pound calamari tubes, cut into rings

CORVINA

½ pound skinless corvina, cut into ½-inch cubes

1 tablespoon kosher salt, divided

1 cup fresh lime juice, divided

½ red onion, peeled and julienned

1 cup Nuevo Sauce (page 162)

2 tablespoons chopped fresh cilantro

½ cup diced Sweet Potato (page 134)

½ cup Choclo (page xxxiii)

1 tablespoon Merken Oil (page 22)

½ cup Maiz Chulpe (page 162)

To make the Calamari and Shrimp: Add 3 quarts of water to a large stock pot over high heat and bring to a boil. While waiting for the water to boil, prepare a large bowl filled with equal parts water and ice (creating an ice bath). When the pot comes to a boil, add the salt and bay leaf, and squeeze the juice from the lemon half into the water. Add the shrimp and cook for 4 minutes. Remove the shrimp with a slotted spoon and immediately place them in the ice bath to stop the cooking process. Repeat the process with the calamari rings.

To prepare the Corvina: Add the corvina, ½ tablespoon salt, and ½ cup lime juice to a large bowl. Gently toss to combine and let sit for 2 or 3 minutes. Add the onion, Nuevo Sauce, cilantro, Sweet Potato, Choclo, shrimp, calamari, and Merken Oil. Gently toss to combine. Add the remaining salt and lime juice, per your preference.

Arrange 4 plates on the kitchen counter. Divide the Maiz Chulpe, and place on the side of each plate. Mound the ceviche in the center and serve.

What Is Corvina?

If mahi mahi is the queen of our Jaguar seafood, corvina is the beautiful stepsister. Also known as drum or croaker, corvina is a large-bodied fish found in the waters of the Pacific Ocean along Central and South America. Beloved for its mild, slightly sweet flavor and firm, flaky texture, corvina is a staple in Latin American seafood cuisine. Over the years, I've found corvina—like mahi—to be very versatile in a wide range of regional preparations—from Peruvian ceviche to Panamanian fried fillets. Its flesh holds up beautifully to marinades and high-heat cooking, allowing the natural flavors of the sea to shine through while absorbing vibrant Latin ingredients like lime, garlic, and aji peppers.

In coastal communities, corvina is often the fish of choice for traditional dishes, due to its availability and consistent quality. Its popularity is especially evident in ceviche, where freshness is paramount. Corvina's clean taste and meaty bite make it the perfect canvas for the acid-driven dish, providing balance and texture.

Latin American chefs value corvina not just for its culinary properties, but also for its cultural significance. It represents a connection to the ocean and to ancestral recipes passed down through generations. In a contemporary kitchen, I use corvina to bridge tradition and innovation—respecting its roots while experimenting with global flavors. Its rise in international markets reflects what we've long known: Corvina is a star.

Ceviche Mexicano

MEXICAN STYLE CEVICHE

Here's another attractive and delicious ceviche that's ripe with flavor and texture. Along with our lime-marinated corvina that we toss with crisp red onion, cilantro, and tomato, we add our Celia Dressing that's bursting with freshly roasted jalapeño and garlic, with a touch of cumin, cilantro, salt, and vinegar. The combination is sensational.

Serves 4

- 1½ pounds skinless corvina, cut into ½-inch cubes
- 4 tablespoons kosher salt, divided
- 1 cup fresh lime juice, divided
- ½ red onion, peeled and julienned
- 2 tablespoons chopped fresh cilantro
- 2 cups diced fresh tomato
- ¼ cup extra virgin olive oil
- 1 cup Celia Dressing (page 138)
- 1 avocado, sliced
- ½ cup Maiz Chulpe (page xxxiii)

Add the corvina, ½ tablespoon salt, and ½ cup lime juice to a large bowl. Gently toss to combine and let sit for 2 or 3 minutes. Add the onion, cilantro, tomato, olive oil, and Celia Dressing. Gently toss to combine. Add the remaining salt and lime juice, or to taste.

Arrange 4 plates on the kitchen counter. Divide the avocado slices on each plate. Then divide the Maiz Chulpe and place on the side of each plate. Mound the ceviche in the center and serve.

Ceviche Peruano

PERUVIAN STYLE CEVICHE

This fresh and zesty dish features corvina marinated in lime juice—the purest form of ceviche. For this recipe, we add a delightful blend of sweet potato, Peruvian corn kernels, red onion, and cilantro to enhance the fish with added texture and taste, resulting in a tangy, spicy, fresh ceviche that highlights quality ingredients and the careful balance of flavors.

Serves 4

½ pound skinless corvina, cut into ½-inch cubes

1 tablespoon kosher salt, divided

1 cup fresh lime juice, divided

½ red onion, peeled and julienned

¼ cup finely chopped fresh cilantro

2 cups diced Sweet Potato (page 134)

1 cup Choclo (page xxxiii)

2 teaspoons aji rocoto chili paste

¼ cup extra virgin olive oil

¼ cup Maiz Chulpe (page 162)

Add the corvina, ½ tablespoon salt, and ½ cup lime juice to a large bowl. Gently toss to combine and let sit for 2 or 3 minutes. Add the onion, cilantro, Sweet Potato, Choclo, chili paste, and olive oil. Gently toss to combine. Add the remaining salt and lime juice, or to taste.

Arrange 4 plates on the kitchen counter. Divide the Maiz Chulpe and place on the side of each plate. Mound the ceviche in the center and serve.

Tiradito Lima

DELICATE RAW FISH LIMA-STYLE

With our Tiradito Lima, we like to layer the buttery, melt-in-your-mouth tuna slices in a shingle-like pattern to highlight the star of this dish. The beautiful ahi grade fish is adorned by our signature Nuevo Sauce and Salsa Criolla and garnished with Peruvian corn (Choclo), Maiz Chulpe, and Merken Oil. Before serving, we like to enhance the delicate tuna with a sprinkling of salt and light drizzle of olive oil.

Serves 4

1 pound ahi tuna loin, thinly sliced

2 cups Nuevo Sauce (page 162)

2 cups Salsa Criolla Roja (page 32)

½ cup large Choclo (page xxxiii)

¼ cup Maiz Chulpe (page xxxiii)

½ cup Merken Oil (page 22)

2 teaspoons kosher salt

4 teaspoons extra virgin olive oil

Arrange 4 plates on the kitchen counter. Divide the tuna slices and arrange on each plate in a shingle or fan pattern. Divide the Nuevo Sauce and add to each plate, around the tuna slices. Divide the Salsa Criolla and mound in the center of the tuna. Divide the Choclo and Maiz Chulpe and sprinkle around the dish. Divide the Merken Oil and add on top of the Nuevo Sauce. Season the tuna with salt and drizzle with olive oil before serving.

Tuna Is the Star

As an admirer of tuna, I've witnessed firsthand the rising popularity of fresh tuna across the Latin American culinary landscape. Tuna, with its firm texture and rich, meaty flavor, has become a star ingredient in many coastal dishes. Its versatility allows it to be featured raw in ceviches, lightly seared in tacos, or grilled with bold spices and fresh salsas. In countries like Peru and Mexico, tuna has found a natural home, thanks to their access to high-quality seafood and traditions of vibrant, fresh flavors.

Tuna's taste pairs beautifully with the citrus, chili, and herb profiles common in Latin cooking. The acidity of lime juice in a ceviche enhances tuna's natural umami, while tropical ingredients like mango or avocado add balance and complexity. People are drawn to tuna not only for its taste, but also for its health benefits and ability to adapt to modern, clean-eating trends. It's lean and protein-rich, and it stands up to intense seasoning without losing its character. In today's kitchens—including mine—tuna bridges tradition and innovation, making it a favorite among chefs and diners alike. Latin American cuisine celebrates freshness and boldness—and tuna fits that spirit perfectly.

Slicing Tuna and the Saku Block

Have you ever wondered how restaurants like us get those perfect slices on tuna? It's relatively simple. Here's how you do it: Begin by selecting a high-quality (often called "sushi grade") ahi tuna loin. With a sharp kitchen knife, trim any excess fat and connective tissue, then cut the loin into a rectangular block, maintaining uniformity. Once you have the block, thinly slice the tuna for that perfect presentation.

For a quicker result, you can purchase tuna saku blocks. Personally, I appreciate the convenience of the tuna saku block. It's a high-quality, pre-cut portion of tuna loin that saves me time without compromising on freshness or flavor. With its consistent size and texture, it's perfect for slicing or dicing for our ceviche. There's no need to trim or clean—it's ready to use straight from the package, which helps streamline prep during busy service hours. The block's uniformity also ensures portion control and reduces waste.

Ceviche Atun Nikkei

NIKKEI-STYLE TUNA CEVICHE

Here's another tuna dish that bursts with vibrant, fresh flavors. With this dish, the tender raw tuna soaks up the tangy soy sauce and zingy ginger, creating a savory, slightly spicy bite. Crunchy bell pepper and sharp onion add texture and depth, while juicy tomato balances the dish with sweetness. Fresh cilantro ties it all together with its aromatic, citrusy flair. Each mouthful is a refreshing, umami-packed experience that's light, invigorating, and irresistibly delicious—perfect for any seafood lover.

Serves 4

NIKKEI SAUCE
Makes 1½ cups

1 cup fresh lime juice

¼ cup sesame oil

1 tablespoon extra virgin olive oil

¼ cup soy sauce

1 ounce grated fresh ginger

¼ teaspoon fish sauce

TUNA CEVICHE

1 pound tuna saku block, cut into ¼-inch cubes (see **Slicing Tuna and the Saku Block**, page 169)

½ cup thinly sliced red bell pepper

½ cup thinly sliced red onion

½ cup thinly sliced tomato

½ cup chopped fresh cilantro

Sea salt, to season

1 cup Celia Dressing (page 138)

2 avocadoes, thinly sliced

½ cup toasted pumpkin seeds

Tortilla chips, for serving

To make the Nikkei Sauce: Add the lime juice, sesame oil, olive oil, soy sauce, ginger, and fish sauce to a small mixing bowl. Whisk until combined and refrigerate until ready to use.

To make the Tuna Ceviche: Add the tuna, bell pepper, onion, tomato, cilantro, and ½ cup of the Nikkei Sauce to a medium bowl. Gently mix and season with salt. Divide among 4 chilled serving plates. Garnish with the Celia Dressing, avocado slices, and pumpkin seeds. Serve with tortilla chips.

Ceviche Vuelve a la Vida

COME BACK TO LIFE CEVICHE

This ceviche, which is a celebration of Mexican coastal cuisine, is made with corvina, calamari, and octopus for a vibrant explosion of ocean-fresh flavor. The tender seafood is marinated to perfection, absorbing the zesty citrus essence. Juicy tomatoes, crisp onions, creamy avocado, and fragrant cilantro add layers of taste and texture. Each bite is refreshing and bold, balancing tang, heat, and creaminess. Light, satisfying, and irresistibly delicious, our Come Back to Life Ceviche is the perfect harmony of sea and garden.

Serves 4

VUELVE A LA VIDA SAUCE
Makes 2½ cups

1 habanero pepper

1 tablespoon chipotle pepper

1 tablespoon peeled fresh ginger

½ cup lime juice

½ cup orange juice

¼ cup soy sauce

1 cup ketchup

VUELVE A LA VIDA

¼ pound fresh corvina, cut into small cubes

½ cup cooked calamari rings (page 163)

½ cup cooked octopus, sliced in small pieces (page 192)

½ cup tomato, cut into small cubes

½ cup chopped fresh cilantro

½ cup thinly sliced red onion

½ cup fresh lime juice

Sea salt, to season

4 avocado slices

Corn chips, for serving

To make the Vuelve a la Vida Sauce: Add the habanero and chipotle peppers, ginger, lime juice, orange juice, soy sauce, and ketchup to a blender. Blend until smooth. Transfer to a squeeze bottle or similar container and set aside until ready to use. **Note:** The extra can be stored in a sealed container in the refrigerator for up to 5 days.

To make the Vuelve a la Vida: Add the corvina, calamari, octopus, tomato, cilantro, onion, lime juice and 1½ cups of the Vuelve a la Vida Sauce to a medium mixing bowl. Gently mix and season with salt. Fill 4 chilled vintage soda glasses with the mixture. Garnish with avocado slices and serve with corn chips.

Pescado en Vinagre con Pimientos en Escabeche

FISH IN VINEGAR WITH ESCABECHE PEPPERS

Colorful and aromatic, our Fish in Vinegar represents another celebration of coastal Latin American cuisine. The dish features perfectly seared sea bream that's topped with tender calamari along with bell peppers and chilies that are cooked in a tangy vinegar-based sauce to bring a bold, zesty flavor to the plate. The combination also strikes a delicious balance between heat and acidity, enhancing the freshness of the seafood.

Serves 4

ESCABECHE PEPPERS
Makes 3 cups

½ cup red wine vinegar
½ cup Worcestershire sauce
1 tablespoon sea salt
1 tablespoon sugar
1 cup thinly sliced red bell pepper
1 cup thinly sliced white onion
1 cup julienned carrots
½ cup chopped fresh cilantro
1 bay leaf
½ jalapeño or serrano pepper

DORADO SAUCE
Makes 2 cups

1 cup Merken Confit (page 22)
1 cup mayonnaise
Sea salt, to taste

FISH

4 medium or 2 large sea bream
Sea salt, to season
1 cup cooked calamari
¼ cup chopped fresh Italian flat-leaf parsley
¼ cup extra virgin olive oil

To make the Escabeche Peppers: Add 1 cup water to a saucepot along with the vinegar and Worcestershire. Add the salt and sugar, and mix to combine. Bring to a boil over high heat. While the mixture comes to a boil, add the bell pepper, onion, carrot, cilantro, bay leaf, and jalapeño or serrano pepper to a medium mixing bowl. Toss to combine and then pour the boiling mixture over the vegetables. Let steep for about 15 minutes. Transfer the mixure with the liquid to a container, seal, and refrigerate overnight before using.

To make the Dorado Sauce: Add the Merken Confit and mayonnaise to a blender and blend until smooth. Season with salt and set aside until ready to use.

To prepare the Fish: Heat a large cast-iron skillet over high heat. Do not add any oil; keep the skillet dry.

Season the sea bream with salt and, using about ½ cup of Dorado Sauce, liberally coat the flesh side with the sauce.

When the skillet is hot, add 1 or 2 fish (depending on the size), flesh-side down, and sear until golden-brown, about 3 minutes. Carefully turn the fish over and finish cooking, about 1 or 2 minutes. Transfer the seared sea bream to individual serving plates and repeat the process with the remaining fish.

Add 1 cup of the Escabeche Peppers to the calamari and mix until combined. Season with salt, to taste. Top each seared fish with the pepper-calamari mixture. Garnish with parsley and a drizzle of olive oil and serve.

Sea Bream

Sea bream, known for its delicate, slightly sweet flavor and firm, white flesh, has become increasingly popular in Latin American cuisine. Like mahi mahi and corvina, I appreciate sea bream not only for its taste but also for its versatility—it grills beautifully, as in our Escabeche, holds up well in ceviche, and can be steamed or baked with herbs and citrus for a light, aromatic dish. In coastal regions of Latin America, particularly in countries like Peru, Chile, and Mexico, sea bream is often used in traditional recipes where freshness is key.

In Caribbean coastal areas, it's also common to see whole grilled sea bream served with garlic, lime, and tropical sides like plantains or yuca. Its growing popularity in Latin American cuisine reflects a broader appreciation for fresh, sustainable seafood and a desire to celebrate regional flavors with high-quality ingredients. Sea bream offers chefs a canvas for creativity, perfect for how we like to work with the fresh fish at Jaguar.

Pescado a la Plancha

GRILLED FISH—MAHI MAHI

This is one of my favorite fish dishes in which simplicity reigns supreme. Grilled mahi mahi bursts with savory flavor, enhanced by a vibrant blend of salt, paprika, Merken Oil, and fresh parsley. The firm, flaky texture absorbs the smoky, mildly spicy Merken Oil beautifully, while paprika adds a subtle warmth. Salt sharpens the fish's natural sweetness, and parsley brings a refreshing herbal note. Each bite is juicy, aromatic, and perfectly balanced—a celebration of bold yet clean flavors that make grilled mahi mahi irresistibly delicious.

Serves 4

4 mahi mahi boneless, skinless fillets, butterflied

Sea salt and fresh cracked black pepper, to taste

⅛ teaspoon paprika

¼ cup Merken Oil (page 22)

1 tablespoon chopped fresh Italian flat-leaf parsley

Season the fillets with salt, pepper, and paprika. Baste the fillets with Merken Oil and sprinkle with parsley.

Heat a large cast-iron skillet over high heat. When hot, add the fillets and cook until golden brown, about 1 to 2 minutes, depending on the thickness of the fish. Carefully turn over and cook the other side until the fish is fully cooked, about 2 to 3 minutes. Remove, plate, and serve immediately.

Why Butterfly the Fillet?

Butterflying a fish fillet, such as mahi mahi, is a key technique that ensures even cooking, especially with thicker cuts. By splitting the fillet and spreading it open, you create a uniform thickness that allows heat to penetrate evenly, avoiding overcooked edges and undercooked centers. This method also increases surface area, encouraging caramelization and deeper flavor. From a presentation standpoint, butterflying provides an elegant look and even creates a pocket for stuffing, giving you more room for creativity. For delicate fish, it helps reduce curling and maintain moisture. Simple yet transformative, this step elevates seafood cookery and should be part of every chef's and home cook's repertoire.

Salmon Norma con Salsa de Mantequilla y Lima

SALMON NORMA WITH BUTTER LIME SAUCE

This dish is named after Norma, one of our loyal guests at Jaguar. One Sunday evening, Norma came in for dinner and ordered the vegetable medley we had featured on our menu as a weekend special. She loved it so much that when we took the medley off the menu, she requested it anyway. Soon, Norma was ordering the vegetable medley twice a week. We began referring to the dish as Norma's Veggies. Eventually, and to Norma's delight, we put the vegetables back on the menu, where they've remained for more than ten years now. It's also one of my personal favorites. Hearts of palm from Brazil. Sweet potato from Central America. Sweet yellow corn from Peru. A true Latin American classic. One bite and you'll find the textures and flavors to be well-balanced while the char elevates them to another level. In this recipe, we add a beautiful piece of grilled salmon that's dressed with a Butter Lime Sauce for a smooth citrus finish. It's the perfect pairing to the sautéed vegetables.

Serves 4

BUTTER LIME SAUCE
Makes 2 cups

½ cup white wine

1 teaspoon apple cider vinegar

½ cup orange juice

½ cup lime juice

½ small shallot, peeled and sliced

1 teaspoon salt

1 teaspoon fresh cracked black pepper

1 bay leaf

1 sprig fresh thyme

½ pound soft unsalted butter, cut in cubes

SALMON

4 (6-ounce) fresh wild-caught salmon fillets, skin-on, center cuts

Sea salt, as needed

1 cup canned hearts of palm, sliced into ½-inch rings

1 cup Sweet Potato (page 134)

1 cup yellow sweet corn

¼ cup watercress

To make the Butter Lime Sauce: Add the wine, vinegar, orange juice, lime juice, shallots, salt, pepper, bay leaf, and thyme to a small saucepan over medium-high heat. Stir while reducing the liquid by half, about 7 or 8 minutes. Reduce the heat to low and whisk in the butter, one piece at a time, until all the butter has been incorporated. **Note:** The trick is to keep the sauce warm enough to melt the butter, but not too hot because you don't want the butter solids to separate from the liquid. Keep the sauce warm until ready to serve. When serving, strain the sauce over the fish to keep the solids and aromatics from going into the dish. You can also strain the sauce beforehand so long as the sauce stays warm prior to serving.

Preheat an outdoor grill to high heat. Make sure the grates are well oiled to ensure the salmon doesn't stick. Season the salmon fillets with salt and place on the grill, flesh-side down. Cook for 1 to 3 minutes, depending on how thick the fillets are. Carefully turn the fish over and reduce the heat to medium. Cook the fish for 3 to 5 minutes. Remove the fish from the grill and let rest for about 5 minutes (the fish will continue to cook).

While the fish is resting, add the hearts of palm, Sweet Potato, and corn to a large cast-iron skillet or pan over high heat. Season with salt and allow the vegetables to char, tossing occasionally, about 2 or 3 minutes. About a minute before the vegetables are finished, add the watercress and let it slightly wilt.

To serve, divide the vegetables equally among 4 serving plates. Place a salmon fillet on top and drizzle with the Butter Lime Sauce.

Tortita de Cangrejo con Ceviche

CRISPY CRAB CAKE WITH CEVICHE

We love our crab cakes—and these crispy cakes offer a golden, savory crunch that gives way to tender, sweet crab meat within. We then like to top them with fresh ceviche, which adds a zesty, citrus-kissed contrast that brightens the richness of the cake. The tang of lime, the bite of onion, and the freshness of herbs and seafood in the ceviche create a vibrant balance. Together, the textures and flavors form a mouthwatering harmony that's both refreshing and indulgently satisfying.

Serves 4

CRAB CAKES
Makes 4 cakes

1 teaspoon unsalted butter

1 shallot, peeled and minced

¼ cup cooked corn kernels

1 teaspoon whole grain mustard

2 large eggs, divided

½ teaspoon chipotle peppers in adobo sauce, puréed

¼ cup grated fresh Parmesan cheese

1½ cups fresh lump crab meat

Kosher salt, to taste

1 cup all-purpose flour

1 cup panko breadcrumbs

1 cup finely crushed corn flakes

½ cup vegetable oil, for frying

CEVICHE

½ cup Aji Amarillo Aioli (page 32)

½ cup Aji Panca Sauce (page 32)

1 cup Ceviche Mexicano (page 166)

To make the Crab Cakes: Melt the butter in a large sauté pan over medium heat. Add the shallots and corn and cook, stirring, until the shallots are translucent, about 5 minutes. Transfer to a large mixing bowl. Add the mustard, 1 egg, puréed chipotle, and cheese, mixing well. Gently fold in the crab meat and season with salt. Using your hands or a scoop, form 4 (3-ounce) balls. Refrigerate for 1 hour to chill.

To fry: Prepare a dredging station with flour in one bowl, the remaining beaten egg in another, and panko mixed with corn flakes in a third. Dip each crab cake ball in the flour, then egg, then crumb mixture. Cover and refrigerate if not cooking immediately. Otherwise, heat vegetable oil in a large sauté pan over medium heat. When shimmering, add the crab cakes and cook until golden, about 3 minutes per side. Drain on paper towels and season lightly with salt.

To assemble: Spread Aji Amarillo Aioli and Aji Panca Sauce on 4 plates. Place a crab cake in the center, top with Ceviche Mexicano, and serve.

Camarones al Ajillo

SHRIMP WITH GARLIC & GUAJILLO PURÉE

Here's another recipe that's a must—especially if you like shrimp. The secret to this dish is coating the shrimp in golden breadcrumbs and frying them, which makes them irresistibly crispy and crunchy while revealing succulent, juicy seafood within. Melted butter and fragrant garlic elevate the richness, while the bold Sour Orange Cuban Mojo adds a tangy punch. The smoky, mildly spicy Guajillo Purée brings depth and a gentle heat that lingers perfectly on the palate. At Jaguar, we serve our breaded shrimp alongside fluffy white rice. It's seafood indulgence at its finest.

Serves 4

GUAJILLO PURÉE
Makes 1 cup

2 guajillo chiles, cleaned and patted dry

¼ white onion

1 garlic clove

1 clove

1 teaspoon kosher salt

1 teaspoon honey

1 tablespoon apple cider vinegar

SHRIMP

1 tablespoon unsalted butter

20 large (U/12) shrimp

Kosher salt, to taste

4 tablespoons Sour Orange Cuban Mojo (page 220)

1 tablespoon chopped fresh Italian flat-leaf parsley

2 tablespoons panko breadcrumbs

4 cups cooked white rice, for serving

To make the Guajillo Purée: Add the chiles, onion, garlic, clove, salt, honey, vinegar, and 1 cup water to a large saucepan over high heat and bring to a boil. Reduce the heat to medium and cook for 5 minutes. Remove from heat and carefully remove the clove and discard. Using an immersion blender, mix until a red paste-like mixture is achieved. Set aside until ready to use.

Heat a large cast-iron skillet or pan, or wok over high heat. When hot, add the butter and shrimp and season with salt. As the shrimp begin to turn pink, about 1 minute, add the Sour Orange Cuban Mojo, 1 tablespoon of the Guajillo Purée, and toss well. Cook for another 2 minutes then turn off the heat. Add the parsley and breadcrumbs and toss a couple of times so the crumbs absorb all the buttery garlic flavor and stick to the shrimp. Divide all the contents of the pan among serving plates (5 shrimp per plate) and serve with white rice.

Langostinos Encocados

PRAWNS FROM ECUADOR

Yet another favorite at Jaguar, here we feature grilled prawns with chorizo, Choclo, and our Encocado Sauce infused with coconut milk to create a rich, vibrant dish bursting with flavor. The smoky, charred prawns, with a touch of heat from our Dorado Sauce, pair perfectly with the spicy, savory chorizo, while the corn adds crunch and freshness and the coconut ties everything together with its creamy, tropical warmth, balancing the heat and enhancing the shrimp's natural sweetness. If you're ready for an unforgettable combination that feels indulgent yet bright, you'll want to make this dish.

Serves 4

ENCOCADO SAUCE
Makes 2 cups

1 tablespoon unsalted butter

1 clove garlic

1 cup finely chopped white onion

1 cup dry white wine

1 bay leaf

Kosher salt, to taste

1 (13.5-ounce) can coconut milk

PRAWNS

16 large (U/7) shrimp, head on with tail shell removed

Kosher salt, to taste

½ cup Dorado Sauce (page <OV>)

1 cup chorizo

1 cup cooked Choclo (page xxxiii)

¼ cup chopped fresh cilantro

To make the Encocado Sauce: Melt the butter in a large saucepan over low heat. Add the garlic and onion and cook until soft, about 15 minutes. Add the wine, bay leaf, and a pinch of salt. Reduce until the wine is almost gone. Add the coconut milk, raise the heat to medium, bring to a boil, then turn off the heat. Remove the bay leaf and blend with an immersion blender until smooth. Adjust seasoning and set aside.

To make the Prawns: Season the shrimp with salt and toss in a bowl with the Dorado Sauce. Heat a grill to high. Add the shrimp and cook 1 minute on one side. Flip and cook until done and heads are crisp, about 3 minutes. Remove and set aside.

Add the chorizo to a cast-iron skillet over medium heat. Cook until golden. Add the Choclo and cook for 2 minutes, until lightly charred. Stir in the cilantro.

Divide the chorizo-corn mixture among 4 plates. Spoon ½ cup Encocado Sauce around each. Top with 4 shrimp and serve.

Shrimping in Ecuador

Ecuador, believe it or not, is one of the world's leading producers of farm-raised shrimp, and its Pacific coastline offers an ideal environment for sustainable aquaculture. I traveled to the coastal province of Guayas, where expansive shrimp farms stretch across the horizon, and the process is a fascinating blend of tradition and technology.

Shrimping here is both an industry and a way of life. I met local workers who have been involved in the trade for generations. Their knowledge is deeply rooted in the tides, the health of the mangroves, and the nuances of water quality. These farms use eco-conscious practices, minimizing antibiotic use and supporting mangrove reforestation efforts.

Tasting shrimp harvested that morning—sweet, firm, and briny—reminded me why I seek out origin stories for every dish I serve. Back at Jaguar, we like to highlight Ecuadorian shrimp in both ceviche and grilled as in our Langostinos Encocados. Knowing the care and craftsmanship behind each shrimp transforms it from just an ingredient to a story of place and people. It's a privilege to translate that journey onto a plate for our guests.

Pulpo a la Plancha

OCTOPUS WITH MERKEN & AJI AMARILLO AIOLI

What a terrific way to wrap up the seafood chapter with a fabulous recipe for grilled octopus. At Jaguar, our guests find our octopus extremely tender and charred to perfection, while bursting with smoky depth enhanced by aromatic thyme. Grilling the tentacles is key because that's what creates those crisp edges around the succulent flesh. The vibrant Aji Amarillo Aioli adds a bold, citrusy heat that awakens the palate, while our Merken Confit, rich with smoked chili and spice, infuses a lingering warmth. Together, these elements create a symphony of flavor—earthy, fiery, and fresh—turning every mouthful into a celebration of bold seafood goodness.

Serves 4

- 2 large russet potatoes
- 1 (4- to 6-pound) cooked octopus
- 2 tablespoons vegetable oil
- Kosher salt, as needed
- 6 fresh thyme sprigs
- ½ cup Aji Amarillo Aioli (page 32)
- ½ cup Merken Confit (page 22)

Fill a saucepot with salted water and bring to a boil over high heat. When boiling, add the potatoes and lower the heat to simmering. Cook the potatoes until they are fork tender, about 14 minutes. Remove from the heat but leave the potatoes in the water until cooled. Then remove the potatoes, cut in half lengthwise, and set aside.

Remove the head from the octopus and separate the tentacles with a knife. Heat a large cast-iron skillet or pan over medium high heat and add the oil and salt. Place the potatoes, flesh-side down, on the skillet or pan and cook until crispy and golden brown, about 10 minutes. While the potatoes are cooking, add the tentacles and press them down with a spatula or tongs. Let the octopus get golden brown and crispy, like the potatoes, 6 to 8 minutes. Add the thyme sprigs next to the potatoes and the octopus. Continue to turn the potatoes and octopus tentacles to sear and brown all sides evenly while also turning the thyme so the potatoes and octopus catch their flavor and aroma.

Place one-half potato on each serving plate, along with 2 tentacles. Serve with a side of Aji Amarillo Aioli and Merken Confit.

Fishing for Octopus

Octopus fishing holds deep cultural and economic importance throughout Latin America, particularly in coastal regions like Mexico's Yucatán Peninsula, Chile, and Peru. Growing up in Mexico, I've come to appreciate the journey of this remarkable mollusk from ocean to plate. Each region brings its own traditions, sustainability efforts, and culinary methods to the table, making octopus not only a delicacy but a story of heritage and respect for the sea.

In Mexico, small-scale fishers known as pulperos dive into the turquoise waters, often using handmade lures and traditional spearfishing techniques. The fishery is seasonal and tightly regulated to preserve populations, especially the common octopus (*Octopus vulgaris*). In Peru and Chile, where rocky coasts offer ideal habitats, octopus fishing is mostly artisanal. Fishermen use traps or collect them by hand during low tide. These sustainable practices contrast with industrial methods, ensuring higher quality and fresher catch.

For me, sourcing responsibly caught octopus is vital. The texture and flavor depend heavily on how the animal was harvested and handled. I've spoken to fishermen who take great pride in their work, and it shows in the final dish. Latin American cuisine celebrates octopus in ceviches, grilled preparations, and slow-cooked stews, often paired with native ingredients like aji peppers, citrus, and herbs.

Understanding the origins of our ingredients connects us more deeply to the food we serve. Octopus fishing across Latin America is a perfect example of tradition, sustainability, and culinary excellence coming together.

Farm & Pasture

We love taking inspiration from the fertile farms and wide pastures of Latin America to create meat, pork, and poultry dishes that are both hearty and deeply rooted in tradition. Drawing from the rural kitchens of Argentina, Brazil, and beyond, our menu celebrates the flavors of the land with bold seasonings, slow-cooked techniques, and a respect for quality ingredients. Slow-roasted pork, succulent roasted chicken, and juicy grilled beef are just the beginning. Each dish tells a story of family gatherings, open-fire cooking, and generations of culinary wisdom passed down through the countryside. Whether it's our Pork Belly Brazil with Black Beans, Pickled Mandarin Relish, and Farofa, or our tender Chicken from the Coast accompanied by tropical aioli and salsa, we enjoy bringing out the best in every ingredient. With rustic charm and refined execution, we're pleased to honor the farms and fields of Latin America through our featured recipes in this chapter—delivering plates full of warmth, flavor, and soul.

Lomo Saltado

SAUTÉED BEEF TENDERLOIN PERUVIAN ASIAN STYLE

Here is a tantalizing Peruvian dish and a true classic, both in Peru and here in Miami. A fusion of Chinese and Peruvian cuisines, Lomo Saltado reflects Peru's rich cultural heritage. It typically features tender strips of beef stir-fried with onions, tomatoes, and a medley of spices, which is then elevated with soy sauce, vinegar, and aji amarillo, a Peruvian yellow chili pepper, imparting a unique flavor profile. After enjoying the dish for the first time in 1993 at Salmon & Salmon, a Peruvian eatery in Miami, I recreated the dish for Jaguar. There are many variations to the dish, but this one is my favorite. Served atop a bed of hot, fluffy rice and accompanied by crispy potatoes, Lomo Saltado offers savory and tangy flavors that evoke the vibrant spirit of Peru.

Serves 4

PERUVIAN ASIAN STYLE SAUCE
Makes 2 cups

½ cup red wine vinegar

1 teaspoon cumin

¼ cup aji amarillo paste (page xxxii)

2 cloves garlic, peeled and minced

1½ cups soy sauce

FRIED RUSSET POTATO
Makes 4 potato wedges

1 russet potato, cut into wedges

2 cups vegetable oil

HOUSE WHITE RICE
Makes 8 cups

½ white onion, peeled and roughly chopped

2 cloves garlic, peeled and crushed

½ cup vegetable oil

2 tablespoons kosher salt

2 cups uncooked jasmine rice

½ cup peeled and cubed carrots

¼ cup peas

½ cup corn kernels

½ cup russet potato wedges

OTHER

1 tablespoon olive oil

1½ pounds beef tenderloin, cut into 1-inch cubes

½ red onion, sliced into thick wedges

2 ripe tomatoes, sliced into wedges

½ cup + 1 tablespoon unsalted butter, divided

¼ cup chopped fresh cilantro

4 large eggs

To make the Peruvian Asian Style Sauce: Add the vinegar, cumin, aji amarillo paste, and garlic. Whisk until combined. Add the soy sauce and mix until incorporated. Set aside until ready to use.

To make the Fried Russet Potato: Add the oil in a deep pan or pot over medium-high heat. Heat the oil to 325°F. Use a candy or digital thermometer to check the temperature. **Note:** You may need to reduce the heat if the oil gets above 325°F. Carefully add the potato wedges and fry until golden brown and crispy, about 12 minutes. Remove from the oil and drain the wedges on paper towels. Keep warm until ready to use.

To make the House White Rice: Add the onion, garlic, and ½ cup water to a bowl. Mix until combined and set aside. Add the oil to a large saucepot over medium heat. When heated, add the onion-garlic mixture and cook for 5 minutes. Add 4 cups water along with the salt and bring to a boil. Add the rice, carrots, peas, corn, and potato. Reduce the heat to low, cover the pot, and cook for 25 minutes, or until the rice is tender. Remove from the heat and let the pot rest for 10 minutes. Fluff the rice with a fork just before serving.

Add the oil in a large skillet or wok over medium-high heat. When the oil is hot, add the beef and sear, stirring occasionally, until golden brown on all sides and cooked to medium, about 6 minutes. Reduce the heat to low and add the Asian Style Sauce, onion wedges, tomato wedges, and the ½ cup butter. Stir gently until the butter blends into the sauce. Add the reserved potato wedges and cilantro and turn off the heat.

Heat a nonstick skillet over medium-low heat. Add the remaining tablespoon of butter. When melted, crack the eggs into the skillet and let them cook until the whites are set but the yolks are still runny, about 3 to 4 minutes. Remove from the heat.

To serve: Divide the rice among 4 serving bowls. Divide the beef and sauce and spoon over the rice or on the side. Add the fried egg on top of the rice and serve immediately.

Picanha Adobada con Vegetales a la Brasa y Chimichurri Argentino

TOP SIRLOIN CAP WITH COLOMBIAN ADOBO, ARGENTINIAN CHIMICHURRI & GRILLED VEGETABLES

Picanha is a cherished Brazilian delicacy featuring a prized tender cut of beef sourced from the top of the rump. Also known as the top sirloin cap, the meat has a lot of rich marbling that melts upon grilling, yielding a juicy, savory experience. Traditionally seasoned with coarse salt, picanha celebrates simplicity, allowing the natural flavors to shine. At Jaguar, we like to enhance the beef by applying a house blend of coffee, salt, paprika, oregano, and garlic powder. After grilling, we'll thinly slice the beef and serve it alongside grilled vegetables and Argentinian chimichurri. When making this recipe at home, begin by selecting center cut sirloin cap steaks with the fat attached. You can also buy one large roast and slice it tableside, which makes a terrific carving piece for holidays and celebrations.

Serves 4

COLOMBIAN ADOBO RUB
Makes 1 cup

½ cup ground coffee

3 tablespoons paprika

2 tablespoons dried oregano

1 tablespoon kosher salt

3 tablespoons garlic powder

ARGENTINIAN CHIMICHURRI
Makes 2 cups

1 cup olive oil

5 cloves garlic, peeled

1 teaspoon kosher salt

¼ cup red wine vinegar

1 tablespoon paprika

3 tablespoons Merken Oil (page 22)

1 teaspoon dried oregano

3 cups chopped fresh curly parsley

GRILLED VEGETABLES
Serves 4

2 tablespoons Chimichurri (page 110)

8 slices zucchini (2-inch x 4-inch x ¼-inch thick rectangles)

4 slices large red bell pepper (2-inch x 4-inch x ¼-inch thick rectangles)

4 (½-inch thick) red onion ring slices

8 asparagus spears, bottom part trimmed

1 teaspoon kosher salt

½ teaspoon fresh cracked black pepper

4 sprigs fresh thyme leaves, stems removed

OTHER

4 (8-ounce) center cut top sirloin caps with fat

2 tablespoons kosher salt

To make the Colombian Adobo Rub: Add the coffee grounds, paprika, oregano, salt, and garlic powder to a mixing bowl. Mix until combined. Set aside until ready to use or store in an airtight container away from humidity.

To make the Argentinian Chimichurri: Add the olive oil to a small skillet or pan over low heat. When heated, add the garlic and sauté until golden brown, about 3 minutes. Add the garlic to a food processor or blender and add the salt and vinegar. Blend until smooth then allow the purée to cool. Add the garlic purée, paprika, Merken Oil, oregano, and parsley to a mixing bowl. Mix until combined. Set aside for at least 1 hour before using, or store in an airtight container in the refrigerator, for up to 10 days.

To make the Grilled Vegetables: Add the oil to a large bowl and then add the zucchini, bell pepper, onion, and asparagus. Season with the salt, pepper, and thyme leaves. Toss well to coat. Set aside. Heat a shallow pan over medium heat. When heated, add the onion rings and sauté for 3 minutes per side, or until softened and golden-brown. Add the zucchini, bell pepper, and asparagus. Sauté for 2 minutes per side, until softened and golden brown. Be careful not to overcook or the vegetables will be mushy. We're looking for a little color and char, but a fresh crunch in every bite. Remove the vegetables from the heat and set aside until ready to serve.

Season the steaks liberally with salt and 2 tablespoons Colombian Adobo Rub. Add a little oil from the Argentinian Chimichurri and rub it into the meat with the seasoning to create a thin paste.

Prepare an outdoor grill to high heat with clean, well-oiled grates. Add the steaks and sear until desired doneness, about 5 minutes on each side for medium-rare. For medium, about 7 minutes per side. Remove the steaks from the grill and let them rest for 5 to 10 minutes. Slice the steaks across the grain and serve with the Grilled Vegetables and Argentinian Chimichurri.

The Top Sirloin Cap

I love working with top sirloin cap—also known as culotte or picanha—because it offers an unbeatable balance of flavor, tenderness, and versatility. This cut, taken from the top of the sirloin primal, has a generous fat cap that bastes the meat as it cooks, keeping it juicy and rich. It's perfect for grilling, roasting, or slicing thin for stir-fries or fajitas. The beefy flavor is robust enough to stand up to bold marinades or dry rubs, yet it's tender enough to serve medium-rare with just salt and pepper. Economical compared to premium cuts like ribeye, the top sirloin cap delivers excellent value without sacrificing quality. Whether I'm preparing it Brazilian style on skewers or searing it in a cast-iron pan, it never disappoints. For home cooks and pros alike, this cut is a delicious, dependable addition to any menu.

Muslitos de Pollo Adobados con Guasacaca Venezolana

CHICKEN ADOBO THIGHS WITH VENEZUELAN AVOCADO SAUCE

Chicken Adobo Thighs, braised to tender perfection in a rich sauce made from Merken Oil and spices, are bursting with bold, savory flavor. The meat is succulent, deeply infused with aromatic spices and caramelized edges. Paired with our Venezuelan Avocado Sauce—creamy, zesty, and brightened by lime, jalapeño, and cilantro—the dish reaches new heights. The cool, velvety avocado perfectly balances the adobo's intensity, creating a harmony of flavors that's irresistibly delicious and unforgettable with each mouthful.

Serves 4

VENEZUELAN AVOCADO SAUCE
Makes 4 cups

½ small jalapeño pepper

½ cup fresh lime juice

¼ cup white vinegar

3 cloves garlic, peeled

1 cup fresh cilantro leaves

1 cup fresh curly parsley leaves

1 teaspoon kosher salt

3 avocados, cut into small pieces

½ cup vegetable oil

CHICKEN ADOBO THIGHS

1 pound boneless, skinless chicken thighs, trimmed of any bone or cartilage

½ teaspoon kosher salt

½ cup Merken Oil (page 22)

1 teaspoon garlic powder

½ teaspoon ground cumin

1 teaspoon paprika

½ teaspoon turmeric

2 tablespoons vegetable oil

2 tablespoons chopped fresh curly parsley

1 cup watercress

1 cup Pickled Red Onions (page 24)

To make the Venezuelan Avocado Sauce: Add the jalapeño, lime juice, vinegar, garlic, cilantro, parsley, and salt to a blender. Blend until smooth. While the blender is running, add the avocado, several pieces at a time, and then the oil in a steady stream. Taste and adjust the seasoning if necessary. Transfer to a container and set aside until ready to use.

To make the chicken: Add the chicken thighs to a medium-sized bowl. **Note:** If the thighs are too large, cut them in half; or you can also cut the thighs into bite-sized pieces. Season with salt. Add the Merken Oil, garlic powder, cumin, paprika, and turmeric. Mix well, cover, and refrigerate overnight.

Add the vegetable oil to a large cast-iron skillet or pan over medium-high heat.

Uncover the chicken and gently toss with the parsley. When the oil is heated, add the marinated chicken. **Note:** Use a splash screen to contain the splattering oil when frying. Cook the chicken on one side until charred and reddish-brown in color, about 2 minutes. Turn the chicken over and repeat the process until the chicken is cooked through. Remove and transfer to a paper towel–lined plate to drain.

Arrange the chicken on a serving platter and add the watercress around the rim of the chicken. Add the Venezuelan Avocado Sauce to a dipping bowl and place on the platter. Garnish the platter with Pickled Red Onions and serve with appetizer-style toothpicks.

Chicken Thighs vs Chicken Breast

If you ask me what I think is better, I'll always choose chicken thighs over breasts when flavor is the priority. Thigh meat, being dark meat, has a higher fat content, which translates to richer taste and juicier texture. Fat equals flavor—that's a core truth in our kitchen. Unlike chicken breasts, which can dry out quickly and require careful cooking, thighs are far more forgiving. You can roast, braise, grill, or sauté them, and they'll still stay succulent.

Another reason I favor thighs is their versatility. The connective tissue in the meat breaks down during cooking, adding body and depth to sauces and stews. This gives dishes a luxurious mouthfeel that breasts just can't match. In dishes from around the world—from Asian stir-fries to Mediterranean tagines—chicken thighs are the go-to cut because they absorb marinades beautifully and stand up to bold spices and slow cooking.

Chicken breasts are often praised for being lean and healthy, but they're bland by comparison. Thighs offer a balance: flavorful and moist yet still packed with protein. If you're cooking for taste, texture, and satisfaction, chicken thighs are the superior choice every time. They bring the soul to a dish—and that's what great cooking is all about.

Pollo Costeño

CHICKEN FROM THE COAST

Pollo Costeño is one of my favorite chicken dishes. It's a flavor-packed delight, marinated with vibrant coastal spices and grilled to juicy perfection. Its smoky, savory profile is elevated by our Tropical Aioli—smooth, tangy, and kissed with hints of citrus and garlic. Our Tropical Criolla adds a refreshing burst of sweetness and heat, blending coleslaw, bell pepper, mango, and our Salsa Muerte for a bright contrast. Every bite is a tropical escape, bursting with bold, sun-soaked flavors that dance across the palate.

Serves 4

SALSA MUERTE
Makes 4 cups

- 6 cloves garlic, peeled
- 1 cup fresh lime juice
- 2 tablespoons kosher salt
- ½ cup white vinegar
- 12 habanero peppers, stems removed
- 12 chile de arbol, stems removed
- 1 cup fresh cilantro leaves
- 1½ cups vegetable oil

TROPICAL AIOLI
Makes 2 cups

- 2 cloves garlic, peeled
- ¼ cup fresh lime juice
- ¼ cup fresh pineapple juice
- 1½ cups mayonnaise
- 1 tablespoon jerk seasoning
- 1 tablespoon Salsa Muerte
- Kosher salt, as needed

TROPICAL CRIOLLA
Makes 4 cups

- 2 cups Coleslaw (page 58)
- ½ cup thinly sliced red bell pepper
- 1 cup mango, ½-inch cubed
- 3 tablespoons chopped fresh cilantro
- 1 tablespoon chopped fresh mint
- ¼ cup thinly sliced red onion
- ½ cup fresh lime juice
- 1 teaspoon Salsa Muerte
- ½ cup apple cider vinegar
- Kosher salt, as needed

CHICKEN COSTEÑO MARINADE
Makes 4 cups

- 2 cloves garlic, peeled
- 2 cups Chimichurri (page 110)
- 1 cup Merken Oil (page 22)
- 2 tablespoons jerk seasoning
- 1 tablespoon fresh cilantro leaves
- 1 medium white onion, peeled and chopped
- ¼ cup fresh orange juice
- 2 tablespoons fresh grated ginger
- 2 tablespoons sugar
- 2 tablespoons Maggi Seasoning
- 1 tablespoon kosher salt
- 1 lemon, thinly sliced

2 whole "broiler" chickens, with rib cage, neck, and thighbones removed; leg bones intact

To make the Salsa Muerte: Add the garlic, lime juice, salt, vinegar, habaneros, chile de arbol, and cilantro to a blender. **Note:** You likely will want to use a face mask to cover your nose and mouth when working with the habaneros. While the blender is running, add the oil in a steady stream. Taste and adjust the seasoning if necessary. Transfer to a container and set aside until ready to use.

To make the Tropical Aioli: Add the garlic, lime juice, and pineapple juice to a tall container and blend with an immersion or stick blender until smooth. Set aside. Add the mayonnaise, jerk seasoning, and Salsa Muerte to a large bowl and mix well with a spatula. Transfer to the container with the garlic and juice and mix well. Taste and season with salt if necessary.

To make the Tropical Criolla: Add the Coleslaw, bell pepper, mango, cilantro, mint, onion, lime juice, Salsa Muerte, and vinegar to a large bowl and mix until combined. Season with salt as necessary. Transfer to an airtight container and store in the refrigerator until need, for up to 3 days.

To make the Chicken Costeño Marinade: Add the garlic, Chimichurri, Merken Oil, jerk seasoning, cilantro, onion, orange juice, ginger, sugar, Maggi Seasoning, and salt to a blender. Blend until smooth. Add the lemon slices and transfer to an airtight container in the refrigerator until ready to use.

To make the chicken: Add the chicken to a large bowl and cover with the Chicken Costeño Marinade. Cover and refrigerate overnight. Preheat the oven to 400°F. Remove the chicken from the marinade and place on a sheet pan, skin side up. Cook until golden brown and cooked through, about 20 minutes. **Note:** If the chicken is not cooked through, cover with aluminum and continue to cook, likely another 10 minutes. Remove the chicken and let rest for about 5 minutes.

Arrange 4 plates and place 1 cup of Tropical Criolla on each plate. Place a small ramekin on each plate and fill with the Tropical Aioli. Cut each chicken in half and place one half on each plate and serve.

History of Pollo Costeño

Pollo Costeño, a flavorful coastal chicken dish, holds a special place in Latin American cuisine, particularly in countries like Colombia, Ecuador, and parts of Central America. As a chef, I admire its rich heritage and the way it reflects the diverse coastal cultures of the region. Traditionally prepared with chicken marinated in citrus, garlic, cumin, and annatto or achiote, Pollo Costeño is often slow cooked or grilled to bring out deep, smoky flavors. The use of coconut milk or local spices in some variations highlights Afro-Caribbean influences, especially in Colombia's Caribbean coast.

Historically, this dish emerged from the fusion of Indigenous, African, and Spanish culinary traditions, which shaped the broader gastronomy of Latin America. It was a practical recipe too—easy to make in large quantities for family gatherings or festivals, using ingredients readily available in the tropics. Today, Pollo Costeño remains a beloved staple across the region and is gaining popularity beyond Latin America due to its bold flavors and rustic charm. At Jaguar, it serves as both a nod to tradition and a canvas for creativity, allowing my chefs and me to reimagine it with modern twists while honoring its roots. It's a true representation of Latin soul food.

Vatapa de Pollo

CHICKEN VATAPA

Here's another luscious Brazilian dish bursting with bold, comforting flavors. Coconut milk, almonds, sautéed vegetables, dendê oil, chicken stock, and tomatoes coat tender pieces of chicken in a velvety embrace. Fragrant with garlic, ginger, and spices, this celebrated entrée delivers warmth and complexity. We like to serve it over fluffy rice and garnish the plate or bowl with scallions for a deeply satisfying experience that showcases the heart and soul of Bahian cuisine.

Serves 4

- 4 large boneless, skinless chicken thighs
- Kosher salt and fresh cracked black pepper, to taste
- ⅓ cup vegetable oil
- 1 yellow onion, peeled and finely chopped
- 2 garlic cloves, minced
- 1 tablespoon minced ginger
- 1 teaspoon malagueta peppers
- 1 cup cashews
- 1 cup almonds
- ¼ cup dendê oil
- 1 cup chicken stock
- 2 cups coconut milk
- 1 cup crushed tomatoes
- 4 cups cooked white rice, warmed
- Finely chopped scallions, both green and white parts, for garnish

Season the chicken with salt and pepper. **Note:** You can either leave the thighs whole or cut them into bite-sized pieces.

Add the vegetable oil to a Dutch oven over medium heat. When the oil is shimmering, add the seasoned chicken. Sear both sides until golden brown, remove, and set aside. Add the onion and garlic to the pot and cook, stirring often, until the onions are soft and translucent, about 5 minutes. Be careful not to burn the garlic. Stir in the ginger, peppers, cashews, almonds, and dendê oil. Cook for another 5 minutes. Check the seasoning and add some salt and pepper as needed. Add the chicken stock, coconut milk, and tomatoes. Continue cooking for 8 minutes. Return the chicken to the pot and cook until the sauce is slightly thick, and the chicken is cooked through, about 10 minutes. **Note:** If the sauce is too thick, add some additional chicken stock to lighten the consistency. Remove from the heat.

To serve, divide the cooked rice among 4 serving plates or bowls. Spoon the chicken and sauce over the top. Garnish with the scallions and serve.

Panceta de Cerdo Brasileña con Frijoles Negros, Mandarina Encurtida, y Farofa

PORK BELLY BRAZIL WITH BLACK BEANS, PICKLED MANDARIN RELISH & FAROFA

Get ready for an explosion of rich, vibrant flavors with this Brazilian pork belly dish. The crisp belly is melt-in-your-mouth tender while offering a satisfying crunch. Earthy black beans provide a hearty base, beautifully contrasted by the tangy sweetness of the Pickled Mandarin Relish. We'll then add Farofa (a cassava flour dish) for a nutty, toasted texture, tying the dish together with its savory depth. Try it and you'll discover a harmonious balance of flavor, texture, and Brazilian soul.

Serves 4

PORK BELLY
Makes about 4 (4-ounce) pieces

1½ pounds pork belly, center cut

Kosher salt and fresh cracked black pepper, to season

1 white onion, peeled and cut into thick rings

10 sprigs fresh thyme

1 bay leaf

1 cup white wine

1 cup chicken stock

PICKLED MANDARIN RELISH
Makes 2½ cups

1 cup mandarin orange segments

1 cup Coleslaw (page 58)

½ cup Pickled Red Onions with pickling liquid (page 24)

2 tablespoons Sour Orange Cuban Mojo (page 220)

Kosher salt, to taste

FAROFA
Makes 2 cups

½ cup unsalted butter

1 cup finely chopped white onion

2 cups Yoki Farofa

½ cup pine nuts

2 cups cooked Black Beans (page 48)

½ cup chopped fresh Italian flat-leaf parsley

To make the Pork Belly: Preheat the oven to 350°F. Clean and trim the pork belly, leaving a generous sliver of fat on top. Score the fat in a diamond pattern to better render the fat. Season generously with salt and pepper.

Add the onions to the bottom of a Dutch oven, making an even layer. Top the onions with the thyme and bay leaf. Place the pork belly on top followed by the wine and chicken stock. Roast in the oven, uncovered, for 1 hour. Lower the temperature to 250°F and cover. Continue roasting for another 1½ hours. Remove and let the Dutch oven cool down. When cool, place in the refrigerator overnight. The next day, bring the contents to room temperature and strain the remaining juices, reserving the liquid in the refrigerator for up to 3 days. Remove the pork and cut into 4 equal pieces and set aside.

To make the Pickled Mandarin Relish: Add the mandarin segments, Coleslaw, and Pickled Red Onions with their liquid to a medium bowl. Mix well and season with salt, to taste. Let marinate for at least 30 minutes at room temperature, then add the Sour Orange Cuban Mojo and mix well. Season with salt, if needed, and refrigerate until ready to serve.

To make the Farofa: Add the butter to a large cast-iron skillet or pan over medium heat. When the butter has melted, add the onions and sauté until translucent and lightly golden brown, 8 to 10 minutes. Add the farofa and pine nuts and continue cooking for 10 minutes, or until the farofa and pine nuts are golden and impart a roasted aroma and the texture is crispy and dry. Set aside.

Heat the Black Beans in a saucepan, making sure they boil only once. Keep warm.

Place the pork pieces in a cast-iron skillet over medium-high heat and heat the pork pieces, turning occasionally, until crispy and hot.

To serve, spoon about ½ cup of Black Beans on each of 4 serving plates. Place the pork on top or to the side of the beans. Top the pork with about ½ cup of the Pickled Mandarin Relish, sprinkle about ¼ cup of Farofa around the beans, garnish with parsley, and serve.

A Note About Pork Belly

Pork belly, a wonderful ingredient that holds a special place in the Jaguar kitchen, has historically been a central protein in Latin America since the Spanish introduced pigs to the region in the 16th century. Over time, pork belly—prized for its rich layers of meat and fat—became a staple in many households due to its affordability and flavor.

Each country has its unique way of preparing pork belly. In Colombia, it's a star ingredient in bandeja paisa, where it's fried to crispy perfection. In Mexico, it's found in tacos de chicharrón, where the pork belly is slow-cooked or fried until it reaches a crunchy, melt-in-your-mouth texture. Cuban cuisine showcases it in dishes like lechón asado, where it's marinated and roasted, highlighting its succulent flavor.

What makes pork belly so beloved is its versatility—it can be braised, fried, grilled, or roasted. Its intense, savory richness pairs beautifully with native ingredients like plantains, yuca, and salsas. Today, it continues to gain popularity not only in traditional dishes but also in modern Latin fusion cuisine.

Pernil con Mojo Cubano y Salsa de Guayaba

PORK WITH CUBAN MOJO & GUAVA SAUCE

Slow-roasted pork shoulder is a culinary marvel at Jaguar. A dish that embodies tender perfection. We like to heighten the succulent pork with the tangy zest of our Sour Orange Cuban Mojo and our sweet Guava Sauce. Accompanied by golden brown yuca fries that are crispy on the outside yet creamy within, the vegetable offers a satisfying contrast to the roasted pork. This is one of the most requested meat dishes on our menu, which doesn't come as a surprise. The marriage of textures elevates the dish to sublime heights, while each bite indulges in the richness of tradition and the vibrancy of Cuban cuisine, creating an unforgettable dining experience.

Serves 4

SOUR ORANGE CUBAN MOJO
Makes 2 cups

1 cup olive oil

½ white onion, peeled and finely minced

15 garlic cloves, peeled and minced

½ habanero pepper, cut in half

¼ cup fresh lime juice

¼ cup fresh orange juice

1 tablespoon apple cider vinegar

1 teaspoon cumin

1 teaspoon oregano

1 teaspoon black peppercorns

1 tablespoon kosher salt

CRISPY YUCA FRIES
Makes enough for 4 servings

2 cups canola oil

2 (14-ounce) cans Goya Yuca, drained

PORK SHOULDER

1 (4-pound) pork shoulder

1 tablespoon kosher salt

1 tablespoon paprika

1 cup fresh curly parsley, roughly chopped

1 cup fresh cilantro, roughly chopped

2 red bell peppers, cored, seeded, and roughly chopped

8 cloves garlic, peeled

½ cup white vinegar

8 cups orange juice

8 cups water

GUAVA SAUCE
Makes 2 quarts

1 quart Pork Shoulder braising liquid, strained

1 quart Frozen Fresh Guava Purée

½ cup white vinegar

OTHER

¼ cup Pickled Red Onions (page 24)

2 tablespoons watercress

To make the Sour Orange Cuban Mojo: Add the oil to a small saucepot over low heat. When the oil is heated, add the onions and garlic and sauté until the vegetables are soft and golden, about 5 minutes. Remove from the heat and add the habanero, lime juice, orange juice, vinegar, cumin, oregano, peppercorns, and salt. Mix well to combine, and store in an airtight container in the refrigerator until ready to use, for up to 10 days.

To make the Crispy Yuca Fries: Add the oil to a deep pan or pot over medium-high heat. Heat the oil to 325°F. Use a candy thermometer to check the temperature. **Note:** You may need to reduce the heat if the oil gets above 325°F. While the oil is heating, cut the canned yuca into triangles or french-fry shapes. Carefully add the yuca and fry until golden brown and crispy, about 7 minutes. Remove from the oil and drain the wedges on paper towels. Keep warm until ready to use.

To make the Pork Shoulder: Preheat the oven to 350°F.

Rinse and pat dry the pork shoulder. Season the pork on all sides with salt and paprika. Transfer the pork to a roasting pan or place in a 6-quart Dutch oven with lid. Set aside.

Add the parsley, cilantro, bell peppers, garlic, vinegar, orange juice, and water to a food processor or blender. Blend until smooth, then pour over the pork shoulder. Place the pork in the preheated oven and roast for 3½ hours or until fork tender. **Note:** If the pork doesn't achieve a golden-brown exterior, remove the lid and continue to roast for 20 minutes, or until the color is achieved. Remove the pork from the oven and let cool in the liquid to room temperature. **Note:** Strain and reserve 1 quart of the braising liquid to use in the Guava Sauce.

To make the Guava Sauce: Add the braising liquid, guava purée, and vinegar to a blender and blend until fully incorporated. Transfer to a saucepot over low heat and keep warm until ready to use.

To assemble: Pour the Guava Sauce in the middle of a large serving bowl. Arrange the Crispy Yuca Fries on top of the sauce. Mound the pork on top of the fries. Drizzle the Sour Orange Cuban Mojo around the pork and fries, place the Pickled Red Onions and watercress on top of the pork, and serve.

SWEET DELIGHTS

As a fitting conclusion to the meal—and cookbook—this final chapter brings the sweet side of Latin America to life with a vibrant array of traditional and reimagined desserts that celebrate the region's rich culinary heritage. Drawing from a mosaic of cultures and flavors, our confectionary creations highlight native ingredients like coconut, vanilla, chocolate, and banana. From our moist and delicious bread pudding and Cheesecake with Hazelnut Brittle to our rich Banana and Crème Stuffed Crepes and Crème Brûlée made with Maize, each sweet delight reflects the warmth, creativity, and joy of Latin American kitchens. At Jaguar, we blend time-honored recipes with our own unique flair, crafting sweets that are as visually stunning as they are tempting. Whether inspired by street vendors, family gatherings, or festive celebrations, every treat we share is made with heart and tradition. With each bite, we invite you to savor the comforting, indulgent flavors that have brought people together for generations. Our desserts are more than just sweets—they're a celebration of culture, memory, and heavenly delight.

Budin de Pan "Gloria" con Nueces Garapiñadas

BREAD PUDDING GLORIA WITH SPICED NUTS

Our bread pudding, named after our pastry chef Gloria, who's been with Jaguar for almost twenty years, is made with coconut milk, nuts, and a decadent Caramel Sauce. The creamy richness of coconut milk soaks into the soft bread, creating a custardy texture that's irresistible. The spiced nuts add a satisfying crunch while balancing the sweetness. A drizzle—or generous layer—of the Caramel Sauce infuses it all with deep, buttery notes. This comforting, nostalgic dish captures the heart of Latin American home cooking and festive celebrations alike.

Serves 4 to 6

MIXED SPICED NUTS
Makes 4 cups

- 2 cups sliced almonds
- 1 cup hazelnuts
- 1 cup pumpkin seeds
- ½ cup sugar
- ¼ cup Cointreau (or triple sec)
- ⅛ teaspoon cayenne pepper, or to taste

CARAMEL SAUCE
Makes 3 cups

- 2 cups sugar
- 4 tablespoons unsalted butter
- 1 teaspoon vanilla extract
- 1 cup heavy cream
- ⅛ teaspoon kosher salt

BREAD PUDDING

- 4 cups cubed brioche
- 1 (12-ounce) can coconut milk
- ½ cup coconut flakes
- ½ cup Coco Lopez cream of coconut
- ½ cup cubed unsalted butter
- 4 large eggs
- ¼ teaspoon kosher salt

Begin by making the Mixed Spiced Nuts: Preheat the oven to 300°F. Add the almonds, hazelnuts, and pumpkin seeds, sugar, Cointreau, and cayenne to a large bowl. Mix until combined. Spread out the mixture onto a lined (or greased) baking sheet and toast in the oven until golden and firm, about 15 minutes. Let cool and break into desired pieces or clusters as needed. Set aside.

To make the Caramel Sauce: Add the sugar to a large saucepot over medium heat and allow the sugar to cook until fully dissolved and amber in color. Do not stir while the sugar cooks. **Note:** Be careful with this recipe; hot sugar can be dangerous if touched with bare hands. When the sugar is cooked, carefully add the butter, vanilla, heavy cream, and salt, and mix carefully. Remove from the heat and allow to cool to room temperature.

To make the Bread Pudding: Preheat the oven to 275°F.

Add the brioche, coconut milk, coconut flakes, Coco Lopez, butter, eggs, ½ cup Mixed Spiced Nuts, and salt to a large bowl. Mix well until combined, then transfer to a greased ovenproof casserole dish. Bake for 90 minutes or until firm and toasted on the outside. Remove and cut into 4 to 6 even pieces. Plate each slice and serve with a drizzle of warm Caramel Sauce.

Chocolate Abuelita

CHOCOLATE CAKE WITH MELTED CHOCOLATE CENTER

Chocolate Abuelita, another Jaguar favorite, captures the heart of Latin American warmth and tradition. Its rich, velvety texture blends perfectly with the bold crunch of spiced nuts, adding depth to every bite while evoking family gatherings and festive mornings. Served with a scoop of vanilla ice cream, this heavenly chocolate cake delivers a nostalgic experience of home, heritage, and indulgence.

Serves 4

CHOCOLATE CAKE
1 cup semi-sweet chocolate

½ pound unsalted butter

6 large eggs

1 cup + 1 tablespoon powdered sugar

¼ cup all-purpose flour

CHOCOLATE SAUCE
Makes 4 cups

2 cups heavy cream

2 cups semi-sweet baking chocolate

OTHER
4 scoops vanilla bean ice cream

Mixed Spiced Nuts (page 228)

To make the Chocolate Cake: Preheat the oven to 275°F. Add the chocolate and butter to a microwave-safe container and heat in the microwave in 30-second intervals until both the chocolate and butter are melted. Be careful not to burn the chocolate. Set aside. Add the eggs and sugar to the mixing bowl of a kitchen mixer with whip attachment. Beat the eggs and sugar until fluffy and creamy, 5 to 7 minutes. Fold in the melted chocolate, butter, and flour until incorporated. Pour about 1 cup of the chocolate mixture into each of 4 greased 8- to 10-ounce baking ramekins. Let rest at room temperature for 10 minutes. Then transfer to the oven and bake for 20 minutes, or until a toothpick inserted into the center comes out clean. Set aside.

To make the Chocolate Sauce: Add the heavy cream to a saucepot over medium-low heat. Add the chocolate and, stirring with a whisk or wooden spoon, heat the cream while melting the chocolate. When the mixture is smooth and all the chocolate is melted, remove from the heat and set aside.

To assemble: Place ¼ cup of Chocolate Sauce on the center of each of 4 dessert plates. Turn over each ramekin with the Chocolate Cake resting on top of the Chocolate Sauce and carefully remove the ramekin. Place 1 scoop of vanilla bean ice cream on top of the cake, garnish with the Mixed Spiced Nuts, and serve.

Crème Brûlée de Maíz con Compota de Jamaica

MAIZE CRÈME BRÛLÉE WITH HIBISCUS COMPOTE

If you've never had crème brûlée made with Choclo, you're in for a real treat. The rich, velvety custard carries the gentle sweetness of corn, while its caramelized sugar crust shatters delicately with each spoonful. Bright hibiscus compote adds a tart, floral contrast that elevates this dessert into something truly special. Try it and you'll discover every bite is a balanced dance of creamy, crisp, sweet, and tangy—an unforgettable twist on a classic.

Makes 6 (6-ounce) servings

CRÈME BRÛLÉE

½ cup unsalted butter

1 pound giant white corn (Choclo)

3 cups heavy cream

1½ cups whole milk

¾ cup sugar, plus 6 teaspoons, divided

8 egg yolks

HIBISCUS COMPOTE
Makes 1½ cups

1 cup dried hibiscus flowers

1½ cups sugar

¼ cup lime juice

½ teaspoon kosher salt

Preheat the oven to 300°F.

Bring 2 quarts of water to a boil and set aside.

To make the Crème Brûlée: Add the butter to a saucepan and melt over medium heat. When the butter is melted, add the corn and cook, stirring occasionally, until lightly browned. Next, add the heavy cream and milk and bring to a boil. Remove from the heat and transfer to a blender (or use an immersion blender). **Caution:** Ingredients will be hot. Purée until smooth, but with a few chunky pieces. Set aside.

Add the ¾ cup sugar and egg yolks to a mixing bowl and whisk until pale yellow. Gradually add the corn purée into the egg yolk mixture and mix quickly to prevent the yolks from cooking. Once fully combined, pour evenly into 6 oven-safe ramekins. Place the ramekins inside a baking dish and carefully pour the heated water in the corner of the dish until the water reaches halfway up the ramekins. Be careful not to pour the water into the ramekins. Place the baking dish in the oven and bake for 45 minutes (depending on the oven and ramekins being used, the time may vary). The crème brûlée should shake slightly when the pan is shaken. It should not be firm. Remove ramekins from the water bath and let them cool completely. Wrap them with plastic wrap and place in the refrigerator overnight to completely chill.

To make the Hibiscus Compote: Add 4 cups of water and the flowers to a saucepot over high heat. Bring to a boil and cook for 10 minutes, or until tender. Add more water if necessary. Once cooked, drain the water and place the flowers inside a food processor. Process until a smooth texture is achieved. Then, add the flower purée, sugar, and 1 cup water to the saucepot and cook, stirring occasionally, over low heat until a syrupy texture is achieved and a path is formed on the bottom of the pot when a spatula is run through it, about 20 to 25 minutes. Add the lime juice and salt, set aside to cool down, and store in an airtight container in the refrigerator until ready to use.

To assemble: Spread 1 teaspoon of sugar over the top of each chilled crème brûlée. Use a kitchen torch to melt the sugar until golden and melted. Once the sugar is dry and hard, add 1 teaspoon or more of the Hibiscus Compote on the top of each crème brûlée, if desired. Otherwise, serve with the compote on the side.

Flan de Queso con Nueces Especiadas

CHEESE FLAN WITH SPICED NUTS

Cheese flan, which you may be familiar with, is a classic dessert across Latin America, celebrated for its rich, creamy texture and sweet, caramelized top. Each country adds its unique touch—some using cream cheese, others adding citrus zest or coconut. The balance of sweet and savory, along with its melt-in-your-mouth consistency, makes cheese flan irresistible. Whether served at festive gatherings or as a comforting treat at home, flan captures the heart and palate with every silky, indulgent bite.

Serves 4

FLAN-SPICED NUTS
Makes 3 cups

1 cup sliced almonds

1 cup hazelnuts

1 cup pumpkin seeds

½ cup sugar

¼ cup Cointreau (or triple sec)

½ cup raisins

FLAN CARAMEL
Makes 1 cup

1 cup sugar

¼ cup water

FLAN

½ pound softened cream cheese

½ cup sugar

1 teaspoon pure vanilla extract

⅛ teaspoon kosher salt

3 large eggs

1 cup condensed milk

1 cup evaporated milk

1 cup whole milk

Begin by making the Flan-Spiced Nuts: Preheat the oven to 300°F. Add the almonds, hazelnuts, pumpkin seeds, sugar, Cointreau, and raisins to a large bowl. Mix until combined. Spread out the mixture onto a lined (or greased) baking sheet and toast in the oven until golden and firm, about 15 minutes. Let cool and break into desired pieces or clusters as needed. Set aside.

To make the Flan Caramel: Add the sugar dry to a saucepot over low heat, then add the water. Stir to dissolve the sugar and don't stir again. Cook until the sugar is amber in color, about 3 minutes. Remove from heat and set aside for several minutes to cool. Then divide the mixture evenly between 4 individual baking ramekins. Set aside.

To make the Flan: Add the cream cheese, sugar, vanilla, and salt to the bowl of a kitchen mixer with whip attachment. Mix at medium speed until incorporated. With the mixer running, add the eggs, one at a time, until incorporated, then add the condensed milk, evaporated milk, and whole milk. Mix until smooth. Transfer to a pouring container and set aside.

Preheat the oven to 275°F.

Divide the Flan mixture evenly between the 4 ramekins. Place the ramekins in a deep-sided oven-safe pan and fill with water until the ramekins are half covered by water. Bake for 90 minutes, or until the flan is firm yet jiggly. Remove and let cool before reserving in the refrigerator.

To assemble: Arrange 4 dessert plates on the counter. Invert the ramekins onto each plate, allowing the Flan Caramel to pour on top of the flan. Garnish with the Flan-Spiced Nuts and serve.

History of Flan

Flan, a rich caramel custard, has a long and cherished history in Latin American cuisine, tracing its roots to the Roman Empire. The original Roman version, made with eggs and milk, was later adapted in Spain, where it became popular as flan de huevo. With the Spanish colonization of the Americas, flan traveled across the Atlantic and took on new forms influenced by local ingredients and tastes.

Throughout Latin America, each country has developed its own unique spin on flan. In Mexico, it's often infused with vanilla and sometimes topped with a touch of orange zest. In Cuba and Puerto Rico, sweetened condensed milk and evaporated milk became staples, resulting in a creamier, richer texture. In Argentina and Uruguay, flan is frequently served with a generous helping of dulce de leche, adding a deeper sweetness.

For me, I see flan as more than just a dessert—it's a cultural connector, shared across generations and celebrations. Despite its European origins, flan has been fully embraced and transformed by Latin American kitchens like ours, becoming a symbol of hospitality and comfort. Its enduring popularity is a testament to its versatility and the rich culinary traditions of the region.

Palomas de Cajeta

BANANA & CRÈME STUFFED CREPES

These Banana and Crème Stuffed Crepes are a delightful treat throughout Latin America, blending rich flavors and textures. The soft, warm crepes embrace the sweet cream and ripe bananas, creating a luscious, melt-in-your-mouth experience. Topped with our Toasted Hazelnuts, they strike a perfect balance between indulgence and comfort. Whether served as breakfast or dessert, these crepes celebrate Latin America's love for fresh fruit and decadent fillings, making each bite a moment of pure bliss.

Serves 4

TOASTED HAZELNUTS
- 1 cup hazelnuts

PALOMAS CREAM
Makes 4 cups
- 2 cups heavy cream
- ¼ cup powdered sugar
- ⅛ teaspoon kosher salt
- 1 tablespoon peach schnapps (or any peach liqueur)
- 2 cups mascarpone cheese, room temperature

OTHER
- 4 (6- to 8-inch) French-style crepes (premade)
- 2 ripe bananas, thinly sliced
- 2 cups dulce de leche, warmed
- 4 large scoops vanilla bean ice cream

To make the Toasted Hazelnuts: Preheat the oven to 300°F. Spread the hazelnuts on a baking sheet and toast in 5-minute intervals until golden and the skins begin to crack. Stir occasionally so they cook evenly. Remove and place in a boiling basket or fine-mesh strainer. Shake to loosen the skins, or peel by hand. Place the shelled nuts in a food processor and pulse two or three times until roughly chopped. Set aside.

To make the Palomas Cream: Add the heavy cream to the bowl of a stand mixer fitted with the whip attachment. Beat on medium speed until the cream begins to rise. In a small bowl, combine the sugar, salt, and peach schnapps. Add to the cream and continue whipping until incorporated. Switch to the paddle attachment, add the mascarpone, and mix until smooth. Alternatively, fold the mascarpone gently into the cream with a spatula. Taste for sweetness and adjust with more sugar, if desired. Transfer to a smaller container and refrigerate for at least 30 minutes.

To assemble the Crepes: Place 4 crepes on a work surface. Spoon ½ cup of Palomas Cream into the center of each and top with sliced bananas. Fold in all 4 sides to enclose the filling, forming neat square pillows. Place seam side down on a baking sheet. Refrigerate for at least 1 hour.

Before serving, arrange 4 dessert plates. Set a crepe in the center of each plate, spoon ½ cup of warm dulce de leche over the top, and garnish generously with the Toasted Hazelnuts.

Tarta de Queso con Crocante de Avellanas

CHEESECAKE WITH HAZELNUT BRITTLE

This beloved cheesecake is another Latin American indulgence, blending creamy richness with irresistible sweetness. The silky cheesecake rests on a vanilla wafer crust that adds a delicate crunch. Topped with luscious dulce de leche and crowned with golden hazelnut brittle, this decadent dessert is a festive staple, celebrated for its balance of elegance and comforting sweetness.

Serves 4

HAZELNUT BRITTLE
Makes 2 cups

- 2 cups shelled hazelnuts
- ¼ cup Cointreau (or triple sec)
- 2 tablespoons sugar
- ⅛ teaspoon cayenne
- ⅛ teaspoon kosher salt

CRUST

- 2 cups vanilla wafers
- ½ cup melted unsalted butter
- ⅛ teaspoon salt

CHEESECAKE

- ½ pound softened cream cheese
- 4 large eggs
- 1 cup heavy cream
- 1 cup powdered sugar
- ½ teaspoon pure vanilla extract
- ½ cup sour cream

To make the Hazelnut Brittle: Add the hazelnuts to a food processor and blitz until coarsely ground. Transfer the hazelnuts to a medium-sized bowl along with the Cointreau. Mix well, then add the sugar, cayenne, and salt. Mix until incorporated. Preheat the oven to 300°F. Spread out the hazelnut mixture onto a lined (or greased) baking sheet and toast in the oven until golden brown, 15 to 20 minutes. Let cool, then break into desired pieces or clusters as needed.

To make the Crust: Add the wafers, butter, and salt to a food processor and blitz until finely ground. Grease 4 (8- to 10-ounce) baking ramekins with butter. Pack ¼ cup of the crust mixture into each ramekin and set aside.

To make the Cheesecake: Add the cream cheese, eggs, heavy cream, sugar, and vanilla to a bowl of a kitchen mixer with a paddle attachment. Mix on medium speed until fluffy and the ingredients are fully incorporated. Gently fold in the sour cream.

Preheat the oven to 325°F.

Pour about 1 cup of the cheesecake mixture in the bottom of each of the prepared ramekins. Place the ramekins in a deep-sided oven-safe pan and fill with water until the ramekins are half covered by water. Bake for 25 minutes, or until the cheesecake is firm yet jiggly. Remove and let cool for 25 minutes before reserving in the refrigerator for at least 1 hour. Garnish with the Hazelnut Brittle and serve.

Acknowledgments

Gratitude for Support and Guidance

I would like to express my deepest gratitude to everyone who has supported and guided me throughout this project—particularly James O. Fraioli and Culinary Book Creations. Your encouragement, patience, and wisdom have played an essential role in every step of this journey. Thank you, my good friend. A heartfelt thank-you as well to photographer extraordinaire Alejandra Urquiza, book designer Jen Montgomery, copy editor Varsana Tikovsky, senior editor Jesse McHugh, and everyone at Skyhorse Publishing, along with the distribution team at Simon & Schuster. Your talent and dedication helped bring this book to life.

Family and Friends

To my family and friends—thank you for your constant encouragement, love, and understanding. I especially wish to acknowledge Iskra Salinas, Belinda Uriegas, Alejandro del Rivero, Diego del Rivero, Bocu, Tania del Rivero, Sofia del Rivero, Julia del Rivero, Camila, and Mateo. Your unwavering support has been invaluable, and I am profoundly grateful for your presence in my life. I am also deeply thankful to my entire family for their thoughtful advice and meaningful feedback. Your insight and perspective have been instrumental to Jaguar's continued success and to the completion of this book.

The Jaguar Family

To our entire team—coworkers, colleagues, and partners throughout the years—thank you. We could not have achieved this without you. The diverse personalities, talents, and skills you've brought have shaped Jaguar into what it is today. While it's impossible to name every individual, each of you has played an essential role in our success through your dedication, hard work, and commitment to excellence day after day. The evolution and creativity born from this remarkable group of hospitality professionals and flavor innovators have left an indelible mark on our Latin American guest experience. Together, we have shared core values that extend beyond the kitchen and dining room—values that reflect genuine care for one another and for every guest who walks through our doors. No lesson has been wasted, and we sincerely hope to continue this journey for another twenty years and beyond, sharing our passion with the next generation of hospitality dreamers.

Community Appreciation

My heartfelt appreciation goes out to the Coconut Grove community and to all our guests from across Miami and beyond. Your enthusiasm, loyalty, and belief in what we do have made this project possible. You have helped us create not just a restaurant, but a true sense of community—a place where food, culture, and connection thrive.

Honoring Our Ancestors

Finally, I would like to honor our ancestors from Latin America, whose traditions and wisdom continue to inspire every dish we create. The ingredients, techniques, and culinary secrets passed down through generations have enriched both this project and my personal journey. To all who came before us and all who share in our table today—thank you for keeping the spirit of Jaguar alive. To all the cooks and chefs who have shared their stories—thank you. Your generosity and dedication to preserving the flavors and history of our culture ensure that new generations can savor and celebrate these timeless traditions.

Index

Metric Conversions

If you're accustomed to using metric measurements, use these handy charts to convert the imperial measurements used in this book.

Weight (Dry Ingredients)

1 oz		30 g
4 oz	¼ lb	120 g
8 oz	½ lb	240 g
12 oz	¾ lb	360 g
16 oz	1 lb	480 g
32 oz	2 lb	960 g

Oven Temperatures

Fahrenheit	Celsius	Gas Mark
225°	110°	¼
250°	120°	½
275°	140°	1
300°	150°	2
325°	160°	3
350°	180°	4
375°	190°	5
400°	200°	6
425°	220°	7
450°	230°	8

Volume (Liquid Ingredients)

½ tsp.		2 ml
1 tsp.		5 ml
1 Tbsp.	½ fl oz	15 ml
2 Tbsp.	1 fl oz	30 ml
¼ cup	2 fl oz	60 ml
⅓ cup	3 fl oz	80 ml
½ cup	4 fl oz	120 ml
⅔ cup	5 fl oz	160 ml
¾ cup	6 fl oz	180 ml
1 cup	8 fl oz	240 ml
1 pt	16 fl oz	480 ml
1 qt	32 fl oz	960 ml

Length

¼ in	6 mm
½ in	13 mm
¾ in	19 mm
1 in	25 mm
6 in	15 cm
12 in	30 cm